FOCUS ON
AQUARIUM
FISH

FOCUS ON
AQUARIUM
FISH

Geoff Rogers • Nick Fletcher

FRESHWATER

INTERPET PUBLISHING

CREDITS

Created and compiled:
Ideas into Print, Claydon,
Suffolk IP6 0AB, England.

Photography:
Geoff Rogers
© Interpet Publishing.

Design and prepress:
Stuart Watkinson,
Ayelands, New Ash Green,
Kent DA3 8JW, England.

Production management:
Consortium, Poslingford,
Suffolk CO10 8RA, England.

Print production:
Sino Publishing House Ltd.,
Hong Kong.

Printed and bound in China.

Photographer
Geoff Rogers has been
involved with aquatic
publishing for many years,
mainly on the editorial side.
This new project has given
him the opportunity to apply
his passion for photography.

Author
Nick Fletcher is a prolific
contributor to aquatic
publications. An interest in
tropical and coldwater fishes
stems from his lifelong
hobby of angling, which he
still finds relaxing. Mainly,
however, he prefers keeping
fish to catching them.

Cichlid consultant
Mary Bailey

Taking these photographs has been a challenge and a pleasure. The challenge has been mostly physical – sitting crouched in front of the tank for hours – and sometimes mental – from the anguish of waiting for some fish to do anything interesting! The pleasure kicks in when the photographs succeed in our aim of showing aquarium fish as living creatures completely at home in an environment quite different from our own. A thin sheet of glass separates our two worlds and yet it is possible to capture the essence of their lives as if no barrier exists between us. This book gives us the opportunity to look more closely at a wide range of fish that many of us glimpse only fleetingly in dealers' tanks. Of course, the fish know that I am there with my digital camera pointed in their direction. The cichlids are particularly curious – look at their eyes following my every movement! And some fish, such as the fancy goldfish, seem to relish the opportunity to show off their finery, moving gracefully this way and that so that I can capture their flowing fins from all angles. Of course, I could not have taken these pictures without the fish and I would like to say a huge 'thank you' to all the aquatic stores and fishkeepers who kindly and patiently allowed me to 'shoot their fish'. The results are on the page – living snapshots of aquarium fish that are true stars in their own fascinating and vibrant underwater world. **Geoff Rogers**

INTRODUCTION

In writing the text to accompany Geoff's photographs, my aim has been to convey the personality of the fishes, rather than to dwell on the finer points of their anatomy or fishkeeping care. I also happen to love fishes. and I hope that comes across. This is a pictorial gallery that provides the 'wow' factor of freshwater aquarium fishes and which I hope will inspire non-fishkeepers to take up the hobby. My grateful thanks go to Mary Bailey: her expert guidance on cichlids has helped to preserve my reputation as a journalist and writer on all things fishy.   **Nick Fletcher**

CONTENTS

These symbols are used throughout the book: ♀ Female ♂ Male

Africa enriches the hobby with a vast array of cichlids which, like their homeland, are beautiful, mysterious and challenging. There is something here for everyone.

AFRICAN

Cichlids, more than any other fishes, have the collective ability to occupy all available habitats – from forest streams to the giant East African inland seas known as the Great Rift Lakes (Lakes Malawi and Tanganyika). Here, along rocky or sandy shorelines and in every level of open water, are cichlids perfectly adapted to feed and breed in very specific biotopes.

The Malawi cichlids of most interest to hobbyists are the Mbuna, which graze *Aufwuchs* (algae) and associated creatures from the surface of rocks. Mbuna do not stray far into open water, and so single species have evolved into distinct geographical variants tied to their location around the lake. The genera *Pseudotropheus*, *Labeotropheus*,

Labidochromis, *Melanochromis* and *Metriaclima* are commonly imported for the hobby. There are also sand-dwellers, such as *Aulonocara*, *Lethrinops* and many haplochromines; and the Utaka (*Copadichromis* and *Placidochromis*), which are typically found in more open water, and feed on plankton.

Almost all Malawi cichlids are maternal mouthbrooders. Permanent pairs are not formed – each male spawns with all available females. The 'egg dummy' markings on the males' anal fins were once thought to encourage females to pick up sperm by mouthing in the

Julidochromis sp. 'Gombi' mouth sparring during pair-bond formation.

right area, but are now considered merely an attractant, males with the most spots being preferred.

Lake Tanganyika cichlids are arguably even more diverse: from the pair-forming, cave-spawning *Julidochromis*, to the mouthbrooding shoals of delicate *Cyprichromis* and their main predator *Cyphotilapia frontosa*, which hunts at dawn

Tilapia buttikoferi – not a great social mixer.

CICHLIDS

A popular Mbuna – *Metriaclima (formerly Pseudotropheus) zebra.*

Jewel Cichlid, a dweller of rivers and streams.

and dusk, when the prey is least active. There are tiny shell-spawning *Lamprologus* species, Goby cichlids, such as *Eretmodus cyanosticus,* that live in rock rubble along the shore, and sand-dwelling

Xenotilapia, in some species of which both sexes mouthbrood the eggs. Topping the food chain is *Boulengerochromis microlepis,* at 80cm (32in), the largest Rift Lake cichlid of all.

West Africa's most popular aquarium cichlids belong to the genus *Pelvicachromis,* best-known in the hobby being *P. pulcher,* the 'Krib'. Small and relatively peaceful, they can be kept in a community aquarium and will spawn in a flowerpot cave or

inverted coconut shell. Do not neglect rapids cichlids from the Zaire (Congo) River. Members of the genus *Steatocranus,* including *S. casuarius* (African Blockhead), have reduced swimbladders and live on the bottom in fast currents. They, and the similarly adapted *Teleogramma brichardi,* are cave-spawners.

There are larger riverine cichlids to consider, too: the Jewel Cichlids *(Hemichromis* spp.) and the boldly striped *Tilapia buttikoferi.*

COMPRESSICEPS

Altolamprologus compressiceps
Mature size: *Males 15cm (6in)*
Females 9cm (3.5in)
Characteristics: *A doleful-looking character from Lake Tanganyika, not cut out for a life of domestic drudgery. The male (shown here) defends nest sites and mates with several females in turn, yet plays no part in brood care. In fact, he would eat the fry if he could get to them. Young fishes make up his diet, and he has been known to egg-rob the nests of other cichlids. But Nature has a clever strategy: Compressiceps exploit rock crevices and fissures as ideal spawning sites. The male is much larger than the female, and so cannot gain access to the eggs – all he can do is fan his sperm into the hideaway. His 'wives', on the other hand, can squeeze right inside, plugging the entrance with their bodies. Both sexes are laterally compressed, a characteristic reflected in the scientific name. This means they can pursue prey in among the rocks.*

BAENSCH'S PEACOCK ✳

Aulonocara baenschi
Mature size: *10cm (4in)*
Characteristics: *This Lake Malawi sand-dweller is found at one location, so there is only a single strain – although Aulonocara species in general are prone to hybridizing in the aquarium. These are the mildest-mannered of Malawi cichlids, so never mix them with Mbuna. The egg-dummy spots are probably just decorative.*

✳ BLUE REGAL
PEACOCK

Aulonocara sp. 'Nagara'
Mature size: *10cm (4in)*
Characteristics: *This fish is probably a regional strain of A. stuartgranti, named after a famous fish-collector and exporter on the shores of Lake Malawi. The lake is so large (584km/365 miles long and 83km/52 miles wide) that it is effectively a freshwater inland sea, and populations of the same species can show a remarkable diversity, each evolving in a slightly different direction. Females carry up to 50 eggs in their mouths for about 21 days before the fry are released. This fish is a male.*

LEPTOSOMA JUMBO

Cyprichromis sp. 'Leptosoma Jumbo'
Mature size: *11cm (4.25in)*
Characteristics: *These shoaling Lake Tanganyikan cichlids
inhabit the open waters of the eastern shore around Kigoma.
They are plankton feeders and, in their turn, important food fishes
for some of the lake's larger predators, notably Cyphotilapia frontosa,
which ambushes them at dawn and dusk when they are least active.*

FRONTOSA

Cyphotilapia frontosa
Mature size: *35cm (14in)*
Characteristics: *The lazy Frontosa picks off drowsy prey fish at dawn and dusk. These are juveniles; mature specimens develop a head hump.*

RED JEWEL CICHLID

Hemichromis lifalili
Mature size: *10cm (4in)*
Characteristics: *The Jewel Cichlid from the early days of the hobby was the very aggressive West African forest fish* Hemichromis guttatus. *The one now on general sale is* H. lifalili, *not quite such a handful but still extremely territorial at breeding time. Its striking red coloration occurs naturally, deepening still further during courtship.*

♀

♂

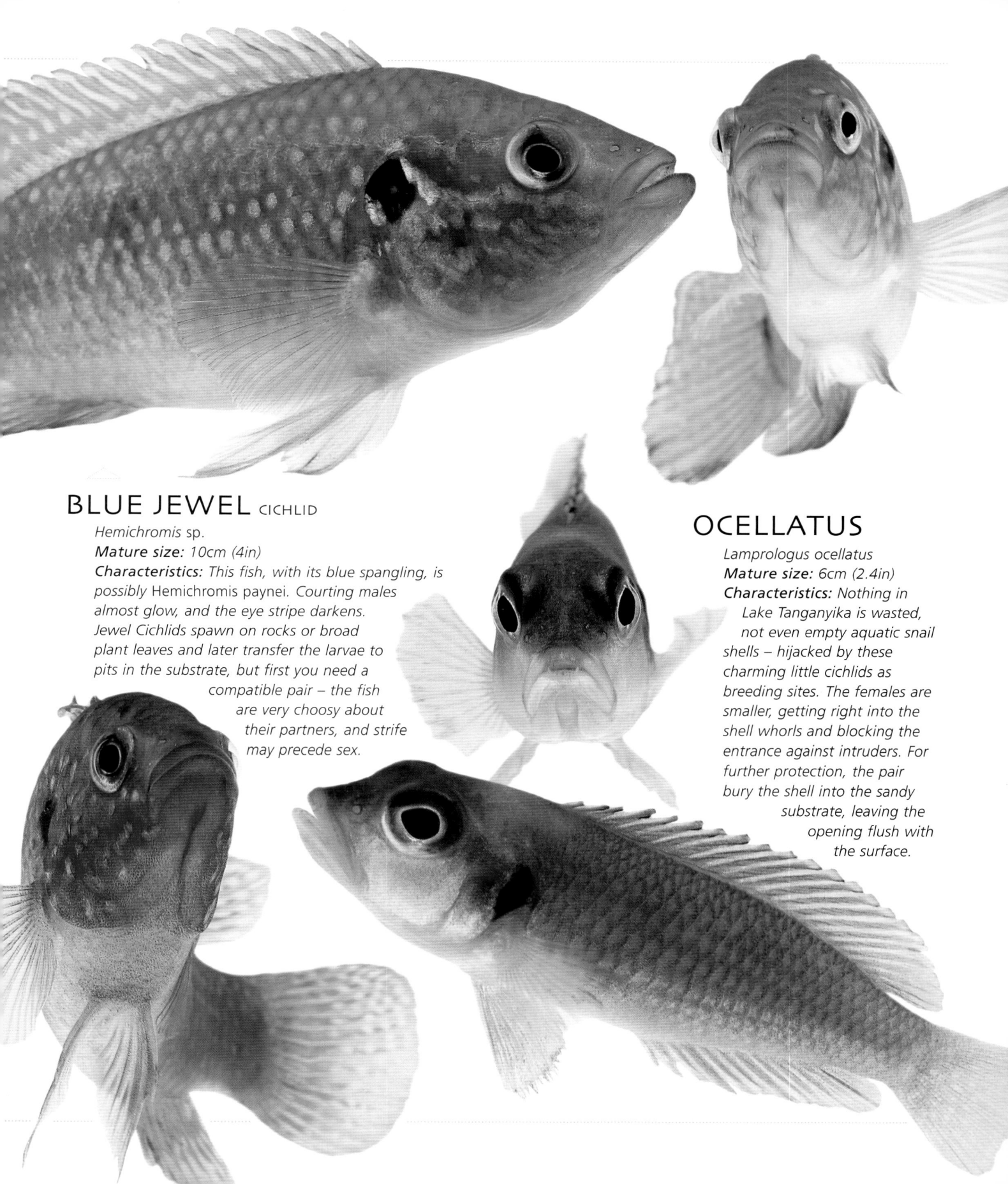

BLUE JEWEL CICHLID

Hemichromis sp.
Mature size: *10cm (4in)*
Characteristics: *This fish, with its blue spangling, is possibly* Hemichromis paynei. *Courting males almost glow, and the eye stripe darkens. Jewel Cichlids spawn on rocks or broad plant leaves and later transfer the larvae to pits in the substrate, but first you need a compatible pair – the fish are very choosy about their partners, and strife may precede sex.*

OCELLATUS

Lamprologus ocellatus
Mature size: *6cm (2.4in)*
Characteristics: *Nothing in Lake Tanganyika is wasted, not even empty aquatic snail shells – hijacked by these charming little cichlids as breeding sites. The females are smaller, getting right into the shell whorls and blocking the entrance against intruders. For further protection, the pair bury the shell into the sandy substrate, leaving the opening flush with the surface.*

GOMBI

Julidochromis sp. 'Gombi'
Mature size: *7cm (2.75in)*
Characteristics: *A pair of these cave-spawners at one end of a large tank, and some sandy substrate at the other for shell-dwellers, and you can have your own breeding populations of Lake Tanganyika cichlids. Gombis make great parents, sharing care of the eggs and fry.*

TREWAVAS' CICHLID

Labeotropheus trewavasae
Mature size: *12cm (4.7in)*
Characteristics: *There are several morphs of this Lake Malawi egg-spot spawner. The droop nose is most pronounced in wild-caught fish. Each male (shown here) should have several females, which are best isolated when seen to be mouthbrooding the eggs.*

GOBY CICHLID

Eretmodus cyanosticus
Mature size: *8cm (3.2in)*
Characteristics: *Living in rock rubble in the shallows of Lake Tanganyika, these fishes have a much-reduced swimbladder and seldom come off the bottom. Males and females share in mouthbrooding the eggs. They look comic and inoffensive, which sums up their character rather well.*

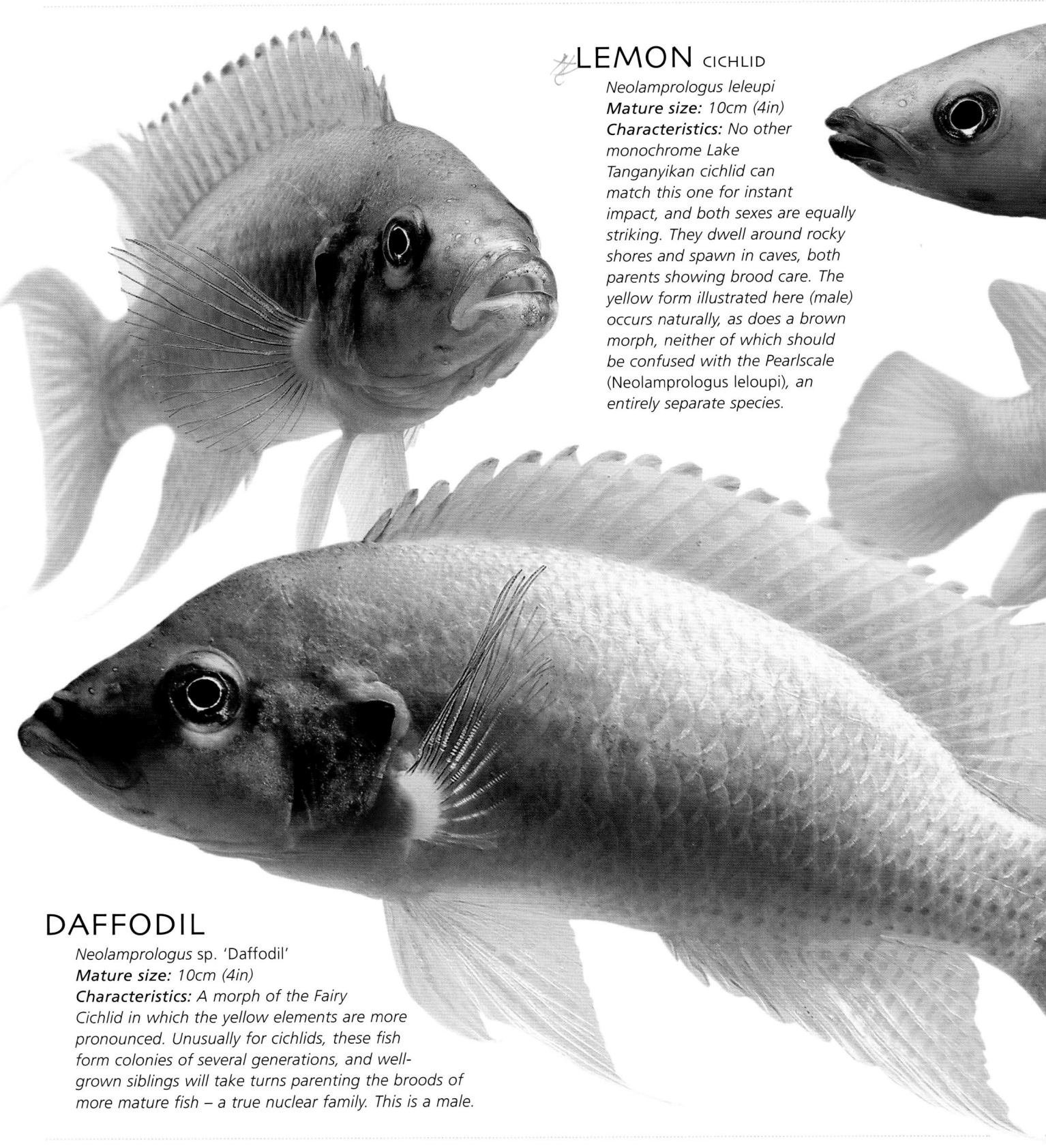

LEMON CICHLID

Neolamprologus leleupi
Mature size: *10cm (4in)*
Characteristics: *No other monochrome Lake Tanganyikan cichlid can match this one for instant impact, and both sexes are equally striking. They dwell around rocky shores and spawn in caves, both parents showing brood care. The yellow form illustrated here (male) occurs naturally, as does a brown morph, neither of which should be confused with the Pearlscale (Neolamprologus leloupi), an entirely separate species.*

DAFFODIL

Neolamprologus sp. 'Daffodil'
Mature size: *10cm (4in)*
Characteristics: *A morph of the Fairy Cichlid in which the yellow elements are more pronounced. Unusually for cichlids, these fish form colonies of several generations, and well-grown siblings will take turns parenting the broods of more mature fish – a true nuclear family. This is a male.*

FAIRY CICHLID

Neolamprologus brichardi
Mature size: *10cm (4in)*
Characteristics: *Is this the perfect aquarium cichlid? In looks and temperament this Tanganyikan species, in which the lyre tail is more pronounced in the male (shown here), is a strong contender – peaceful, graceful and easy to breed.*

♂

♀

ELECTRIC BLUE HAP

Scianochromis ahli
Mature size: *20cm (8in)*
Characteristics: *This gem of a cichlid is found in open water close to rocky shorelines around Lake Malawi. The electric blue of the males (shown here) intensifies on maturity, but subordinate males or juveniles can be confused with the somewhat drab females, proving that coloration is all to do with sexual prowess. In the aquarium, keeping four females to each male prevents him venting his aggression on individuals not ready to spawn when he is.*

BUTTIE

Tilapia buttikoferi
Mature size: *25cm (10in)*
Characteristics: *A banded beauty from West African rivers and streams. House a compatible pair in a large tank furnished with flat rocks and bogwood for spawning. Both parents look after the free-swimming fry. It may be difficult to move these youngsters on – the Buttie has an aggressive reputation – so perhaps this fish is best kept as a singleton, indulgently fed a mixture of earthworms, mosquito larvae and algae wafers.*

DUBOISI

Tropheus duboisi
Mature size: *12cm (4.7in)*
Characteristics: *'Cute' sums up the polka-dotted appeal of young Tropheus duboisi. Who could resist them? Sadly, they have to grow up, and in this instance, the adult coloration does not measure up to early promise; the spots soon fade, leaving a rather drab blue individual with a distinctive white transverse 'belt' down each flank. Nonetheless, these dwellers of the deeper rocky coastal zones of Lake Tanganyika are appealing because they are generally not aggressive towards other cichlids. They are maternal mouthbrooders, and although they have been successfully spawned in aquariums, broods are rather small, typically only 5-15 eggs.*

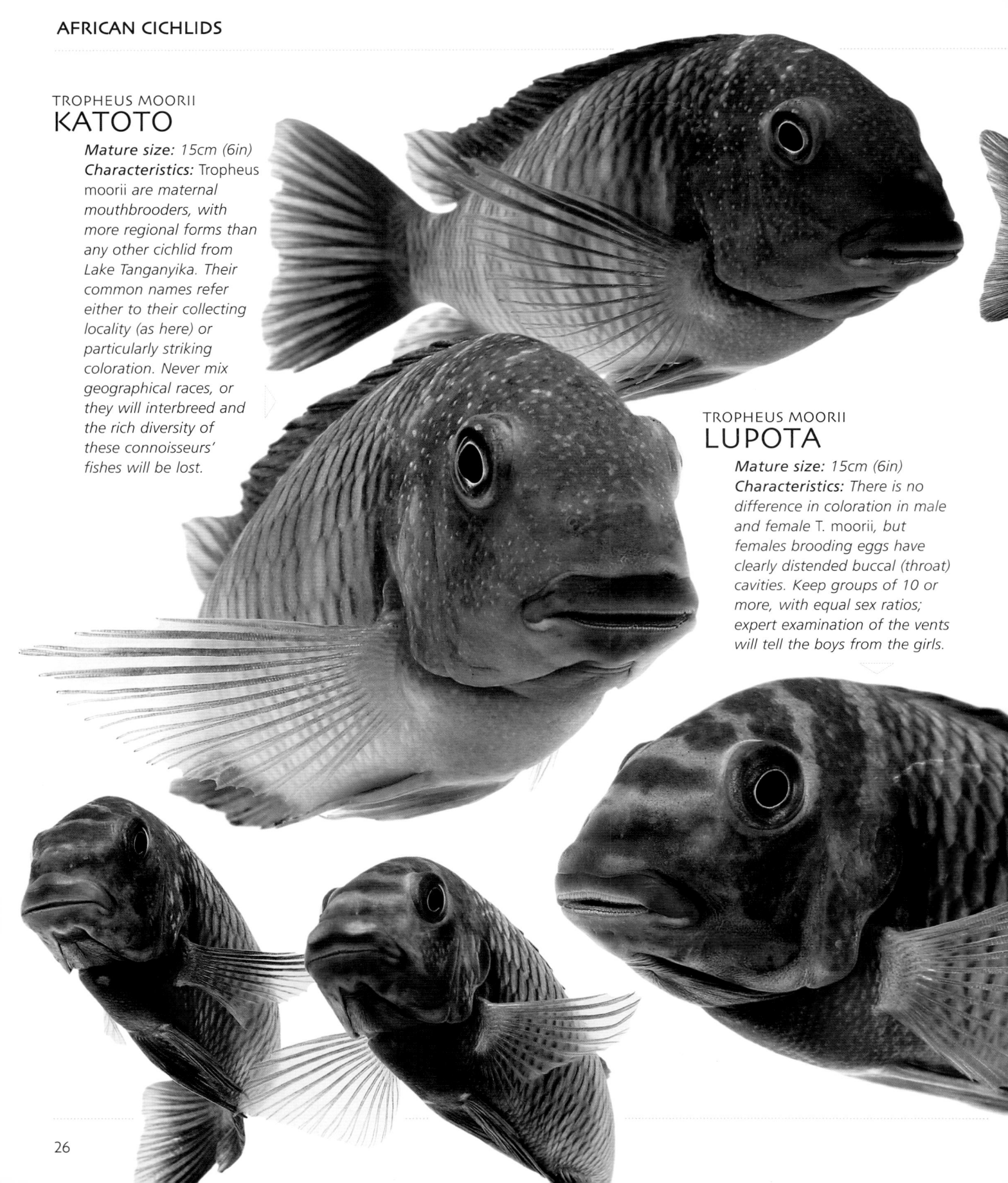

TROPHEUS MOORII
KATOTO

Mature size: 15cm (6in)
Characteristics: Tropheus *moorii are maternal mouthbrooders, with more regional forms than any other cichlid from Lake Tanganyika. Their common names refer either to their collecting locality (as here) or particularly striking coloration. Never mix geographical races, or they will interbreed and the rich diversity of these connoisseurs' fishes will be lost.*

TROPHEUS MOORII
LUPOTA

Mature size: 15cm (6in)
Characteristics: There is no difference in coloration in male and female T. moorii, *but females brooding eggs have clearly distended buccal (throat) cavities. Keep groups of 10 or more, with equal sex ratios; expert examination of the vents will tell the boys from the girls.*

TROPHEUS MOORII
ORANGE

Mature size: *15cm (6in)*
Characteristics: *Possibly the brightest Tropheus morph of all, with the orange flush extending into the dorsal and anal fins and contrasting with reticulated scales fore and aft. No wonder the successful breeding of Tropheus is a lucrative, as well as a satisfying, pursuit – the young are in constant demand.*

TROPHEUS MOORII
CHERRY SPOT

Mature size: *15cm (6in)*
Characteristics: *The double vermillion flank spots stand out to full advantage on these dark fish. Furnish their tank with rocks and sand, and add tall rock outcrops to the back and sides for cover; never mix them with boisterous Mbuna.*

ICE-BLUE ZEBRA

Metriaclima greshakei
Mature size: *10cm (4in)*
Characteristics: *Like many Mbuna, this fish from the southeastern arm of Lake Malawi used to be in the genus Pseudotropheus, and you will still probably see it described as such in aquatic shops. This is a mature male; females are a uniform rusty brown. Always buy wild-caught fish or named tank-breds, never fish from a dealer's lot of 'mixed Malawis'. It is the gene pool that will be mixed, in all probability, as Mbuna will hybridize.*

RUSTY CICHLID

Iodotropheus sprengerae
Mature size: *10cm (4in)*
Characteristics: *Pair-bonding plays no part in the life of Mbuna. Males (shown here) try to spawn with any females in the vicinity, harassing them if they are not ready. A crowded rockwork aquarium, with crevices in which potential 'battered wives' can take refuge, is a good solution to all that testosterone-fuelled aggression.*

South American cichlids encompass everything from Amazonian dwarfs to the stately Angelfish and the endearing Oscar. Central Americans are beautiful, but can be problematic.

Many cichlid keepers will have cut their teeth on the Convict Cichlid *(Cryptoheros nigrofasciatus)*. Long before fashion veered towards the fish of Africa's Rift Lakes, this feisty little Central American was amazing us with its intelligence and devoted brood care. It would spawn anywhere, eat almost anything and put up with indifferent water conditions – but it had another side to its character. When a pair decided to breed, they would claim the entire tank as their own, and woe betide any hapless fish that intruded on their territory.

This is a fact of life with Central American cichlids, most of which are considerably larger than the Convict, and pack correspondingly greater fire power. There are a few peaceable exceptions, such as the cave-spawning *Hypsophrys nicaraguensis* from the lakes of Nicaragua, which will share quarters with the aforementioned Convicts or that other early hobby staple, the Firemouth Cichlid *(Thorichthys meeki)*. But, as a rule of thumb, it is one pair of 'Centrals' per tank – that would certainly apply to the characterful Midas Cichlid *(Amphilophus citrinellus)* or Jaguar Cichlid *(Parachromis managuensis)*.

There is even a case for keeping singletons, which – as long as their owners give them plenty of attention – seems to please both parties.

South America offers a much more varied palette of

Flower Horn Cichlids are manmade hybrids, here shown as a young breeding pair (below) and a vividly patterned adult (right).

Apistogramma viejita typifies cichlid finery in miniature.

A brown Discus, a typical wild type from which many aquarium forms have been bred.

Young Discus feeding on the nutritious mucus secreted by both their parents.

cichlids for fishkeepers. At one extreme are the dwarfs of the genus *Apistogramma*, rarely growing bigger than 8cm (3.2in). These are polygamous cave-spawners in the wild, but pairs can be successfully bred in soft, neutral to acidic water. Unrelated, but still classed as dwarfs, are cichlids of the genus *Nannacara* and the Ram *(Microgeophagus ramirezi)*. At the other end of the size and temperament scale are Oscars *(Astronotus ocellatus)* and the larger Pike Cichlids of the genus *Crenicichla* – beautiful but challenging.

Occupying the middle ground are Angels *(Pterophyllum scalare* and *P. altum)* – often not regarded as cichlids at all – and longstanding popular subjects such as the Festive Cichlid *(Mesonauta insignis)*, Blue Acara *("Aequidens" pulcher)* and

Severum *(Heros efasciatus)*. Amazonia is also home to the ultimate cichlid challenge, the Discus. There are two wild species, *Symphysodon aequifasciatus* and *S. discus*, but many manmade strains have been

developed from these. Discus secrete a protein-rich mucus on which the young feed, and one of the most pleasing sights in fishkeeping is to see a pair with a brood in tow. To get them to that happy state, they will need soft, acidic water of exceptional purity.

MIDAS CICHLID

Amphilophus citrinellus
Mature size: *30cm (12in)*
Characteristics: *Everything King Midas touched turned to gold, but things did not work out quite the way he had imagined. If a breeding pair of these characterful cichlids discovers the golden touch you could be placed in a similar bountiful dilemma, because each spawning can produce 1,000 or more fry. This is a male, with a fatty growth on the forehead called a nuchal hump that signifies he is sexually mature.*

OSCAR

Astronotus ocellatus

Mature size: *30cm (12in)*

Characteristics: *An Amazonian cichlid with personality and attitude, that soon comes to recognize its owner. The Oscar is a source of both delight and despair; cute, entreating babies (shown at top) grow rapidly into rapacious, messy feeders that are not to be trusted with smaller fish. Yet their appeal is universal. There are several forms, including albino, red and tiger. All make great pets, and compatible mated pairs are exemplary parents. Do not feed these fish exclusively on worms. They like them too much and become 'hooked', refusing anything else.*

Tiger

Adult Tiger

Red

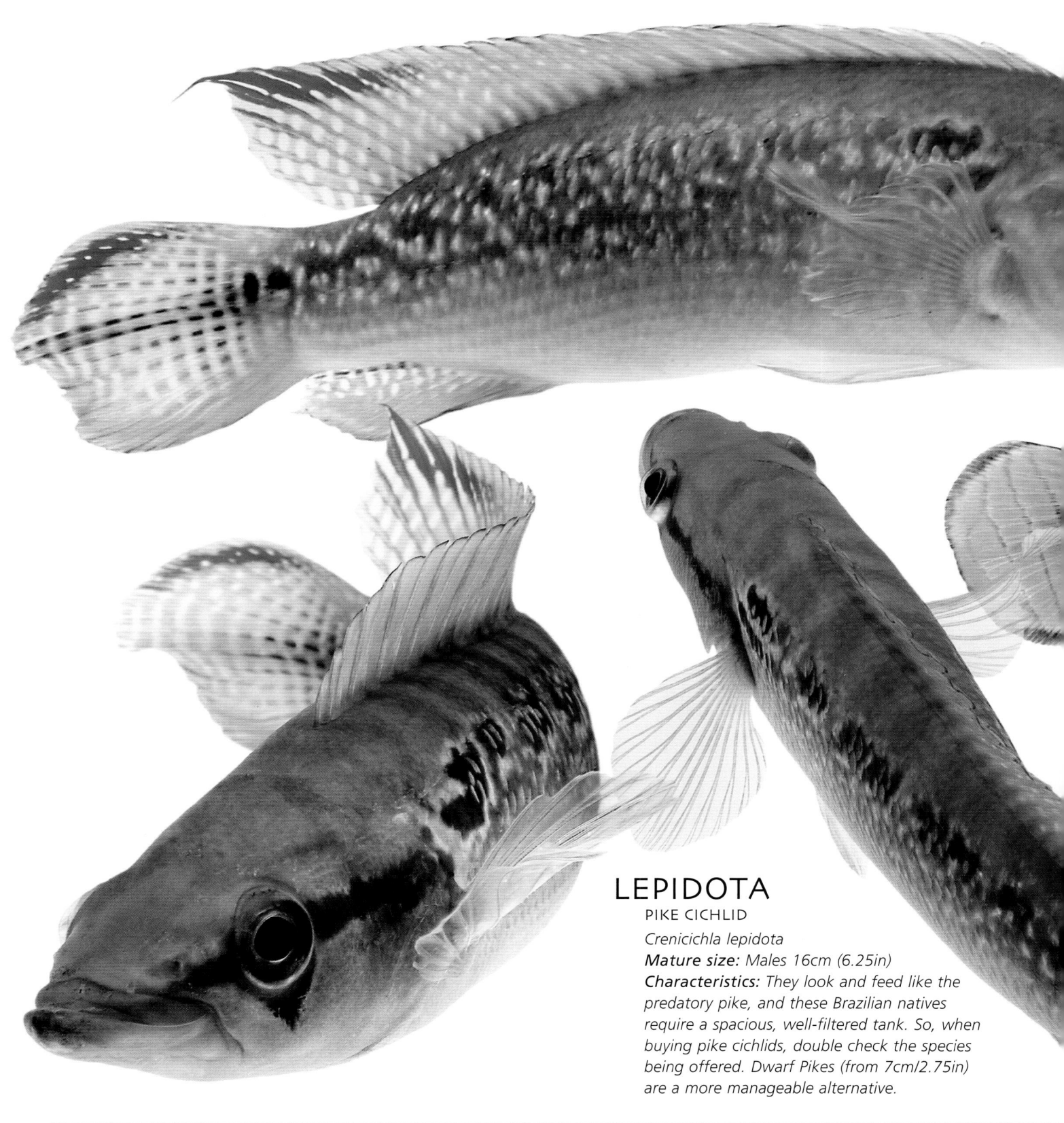

LEPIDOTA
PIKE CICHLID

Crenicichla lepidota
Mature size: *Males 16cm (6.25in)*
Characteristics: *They look and feed like the predatory pike, and these Brazilian natives require a spacious, well-filtered tank. So, when buying pike cichlids, double check the species being offered. Dwarf Pikes (from 7cm/2.75in) are a more manageable alternative.*

COMPRESSICEPS DWARF PIKE

Crenicichla compressiceps
Mature size: *7cm (2.75in)*
Characteristics: *Packaged in impressive stripes, the dwarf pike cichlids provide all the beauty but none of the hassle of their bigger brothers. Fed on earthworms and other meaty foods, these cave-spawners are even safe in the company of comparably sized fish – real little gems.*

SEVERUM

Heros efasciatus
Mature size: *25cm (10in)*
Characteristics: *This open-substrate-spawner from the Amazon and Lower Rio Negro is a very different fish from Heros severus. For years, the latter was assumed to be the aquarium Severum but is, in fact, a mouthbrooder. The mouth-fighting shown here is how potential pairs test one another's mettle. See how the coloration intensifies during the boisterous tug-o-war. Gold forms are common in the hobby.*

JAGUAR CICHLID

Parachromis managuensis
Mature size: *30cm (12in)*
Characteristics: *Many a young 'Mannie' has been bought on impulse after performing an entreating dance like this to an aquarium shop visitor. These big Central American fish are fully aware of the world outside their tank and, given attention, will strike up a one-to-one relationship with their owners, much like a dog. Their lifespan is on a par with our canine companions, too, so a Jaguar Cichlid is a pleasurable long-term commitment.*

RAM

Microgeophagus ramirezi
Mature size: *7cm (2.75in)*
Characteristics: *Mass-produced Rams are pallid and unhealthy – sometimes feeding to improve coloration gives a false impression of quality that quickly fades. This male (right) and the pair below (below) are probably wild-caught or hobbyist tank-breds, the safest route to obtaining good specimens.*

♀

♂

BLUE-POINT ACARA

"Aequidens" coeruleopunctatus
Mature size: *15cm (6in)*
Characteristics: *A rarely seen close cousin to the Blue Acara, this cave-spawning cichlid is found in clear, rocky streams from Costa Rice through Panama to Colombia. The male is the lower fish, showing the more pointed anal fin – not an entirely reliable way of sexing them, however, as older females can also develop these fin extensions.*

♀

♂

JACK DEMPSEY

"Cichlasoma" octofasciatum
Mature size: *25cm (10in)*
Characteristics: *This old bruiser from Mexico, Guatemala and Honduras is named after a former world heavyweight boxing champion, yet is no more pugnacious than most other Central American cichlids; with its jutting jaw and stocky build, it just looks that way. These wild-caught examples have clearly had the best attention from their ringside 'second' – a fishkeeper who has fallen under their rugged spell. In the pair shown at right, the breeding female is darker than typical aquarium strains.*

♀

♂

43

ALTUM ANGELFISH

Pterophyllum altum
Mature size: *30-38 cm (12-15in)
tall; 25cm (10in) total length*
Characteristics: *Much deeper than
they are long, these fishes from the
Orinoco have a sharper gradient from
head to jawline than ordinary Angels.
The barred flanks blend cryptically
into the underwater habitat of dead
wood lit by dappled forest light. These
rare fish are prized in the hobby; if
you can get them to spawn (in soft,
acid water) you are on to a winner!*

ANGELFISH

Pterophyllum scalare
Mature size: *15cm (6in)*
Characteristics: *Many people forget that Angels are cichlids, and territorial when breeding in the aquarium. This is rarely a successful occurrence with the intensively farmed varieties, including marbled (top) and koi (left). They spawn readily, but their parental instincts have been bred out of them so that they eat the eggs. Best success is with wild-caught specimens (right) or first-generation tank-breds.*

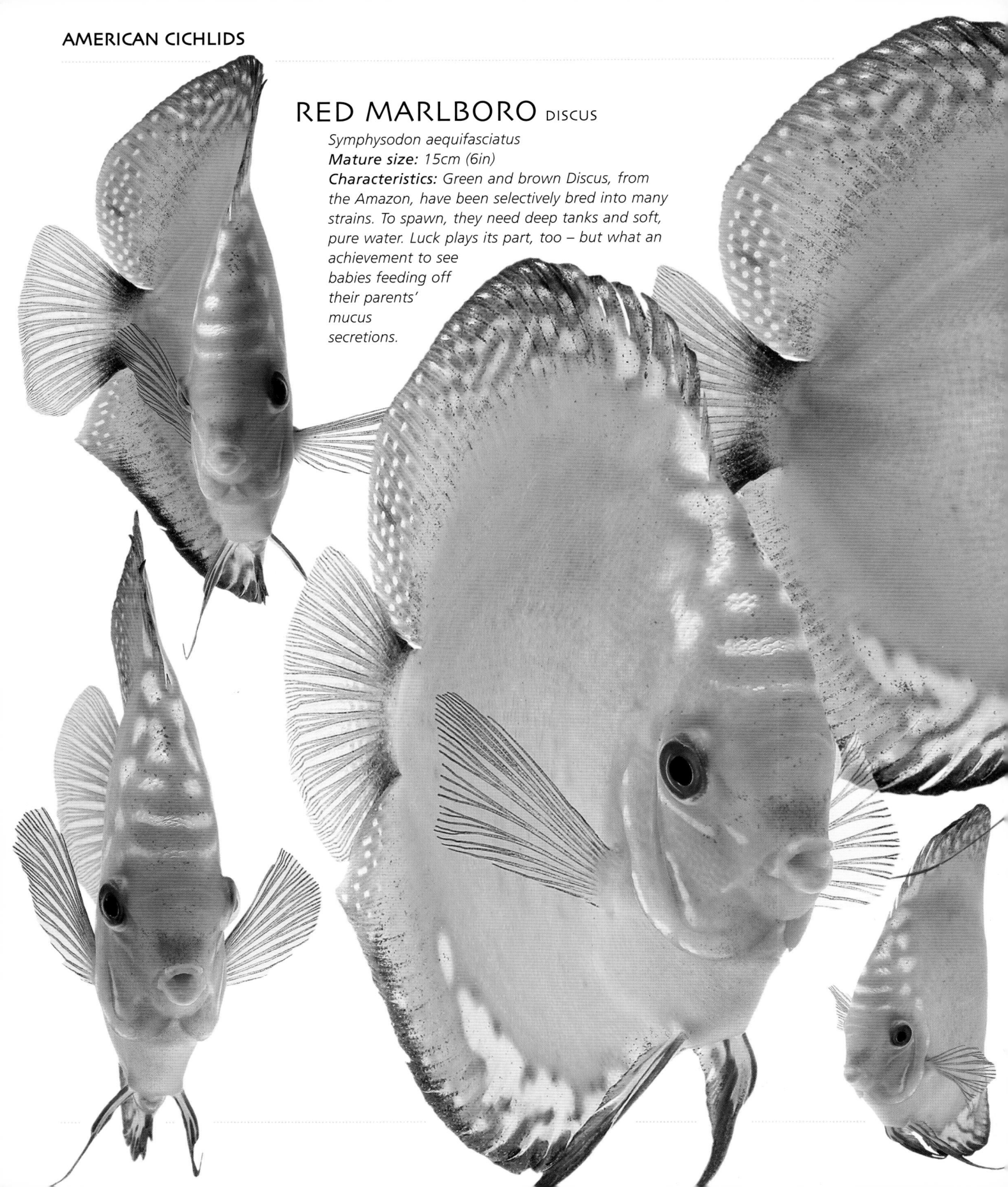

RED MARLBORO DISCUS

Symphysodon aequifasciatus
Mature size: *15cm (6in)*
Characteristics: *Green and brown Discus, from the Amazon, have been selectively bred into many strains. To spawn, they need deep tanks and soft, pure water. Luck plays its part, too – but what an achievement to see babies feeding off their parents' mucus secretions.*

PEARL DISCUS

This fish hangs in the tank like an opalescent full moon, cool and mysterious.

PIGEON BLOOD DISCUS

The term applies to a perfect ruby, but what better description of the scarlet dappling on this beautiful Discus?

SNAKESKIN DISCUS
The blue markings on these Discus are striated into an almost reptilian pattern, hence their name.

BLUE TURQUOISE DISCUS
These fish are sometimes called 'Turks' – a mistranslation of the German word 'Turkis', which describes their turquoise coloration.

BLUE DIAMOND DISCUS

Breeders of this strain are aiming for a single-hued Discus, and they are almost there. Striking, rather than subtle, the adults have a rich shade yet to be fully achieved by the five-month-old youngsters (right). They are of a size to sell on, but keep small fish such as these in groups of at least ten to a dozen. Uniform growth in a brood, with no runts, is a mark of good fishkeeping.

VIEJITA
DWARF CICHLID

Apistogramma viejita
Mature size: *7.5cm (3in)*
Characteristics: *This Colombian triumph of miniaturization shows the typical orange edging to the upper and lower lobes of the tail of the male, which, as in all Apistogramma species, is the larger sex. These are cave-spawners that need very soft, acid water to breed in the aquarium. 'Viejita' is named for its supposed resemblance to a little old lady in a shawl, but no apisto species actually reaches a great age.*

♂

♀

AGGIE

Apistogramma agassizii
Mature size: *8cm (3.2in)*
Characteristics: *A lancet-shaped tail is a common feature of the agassizii group. This fish is a cultivated orange form, with the typical caudal fin shape, but far removed from anything you would encounter in this dwarf cichlid's native Amazonian habitat of streams and pools.*

♂

COCKATOO
DWARF CICHLID

Apistogramma cacatuoides
Mature size: *5cm (2in)*
Characteristics: *This 'double red' form has helped to boost the popularity of Cockatoo Dwarf Cichlids in the hobby. In wild fish, from the Amazon Basin, the tails are nowhere near as bright, and those of the females are rounded. In 'double reds', females' tails can be slightly lyrate, too, which makes sexing the young difficult.*

♀

You could fill an aquarium with nothing but charcins and still enjoy scenes of endless interest. They include universally popular fishes, as well as some for the specialist.

Here we are really looking at two groups of fishes spread across Africa and South America. There are tetras – small, peaceable shoalers, often farm-bred and highly adaptable to aquarium life – plus a diverse selection known as characins. In other words, all tetras are characins, but not all characins are tetras.

Tetras are large-eyed and keen-sighted. Mainly from the Amazon catchment, they seem lit from

A Red Hook (Myleus rubripinnis), one of the 'Silver Dollar' group.

within as their glittering scales refract the light in all shades of the spectrum. Most are egg-scatterers, and show no brood care. They feed on small aquatic insects and crustaceans.

Tetra genera yielding the richest vein of aquarium jewels are *Hyphessobrycon* (Bleeding Heart, Black Phantom, Lemon, Serpae and Flag tetras) and *Hemigrammus* (Rummy-nose, Head-and-tail light,

Glowlight, Golden and Featherfin tetras). But a very small group deservedly tops the popularity stakes on both sides of the Atlantic, the Neon Tetra (*Paracheirodon innesi*) and the even more vivid Cardinal (*P. axelrodi*). These fishes cost a week's

Leporinus species, such as this L. fasciatus, have mouths adapted to algae-grazing.

CINS

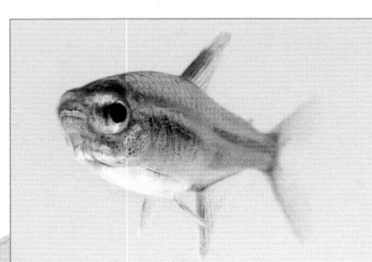

Ever-popular Cardinal (above) and Neon Tetras.

wages when they first appeared in the hobby, but now, thanks to intensive farming, they can be had for pocket money. The same is true of most tetras. Wild-caught specimens cannot be beaten for bright markings, but are harder to acclimatize to aquarium life and require soft, acidic water.

From beauty to the beast – the Red Piranha *(Serrasalmus nattereri)* is commonly kept, despite its fearsome reputation. There are also several convincing lookalikes, namely 'Silver Dollars' of the

Hatchetfishes mirrored at the surface, their 'pectoral wings' ready to fly.

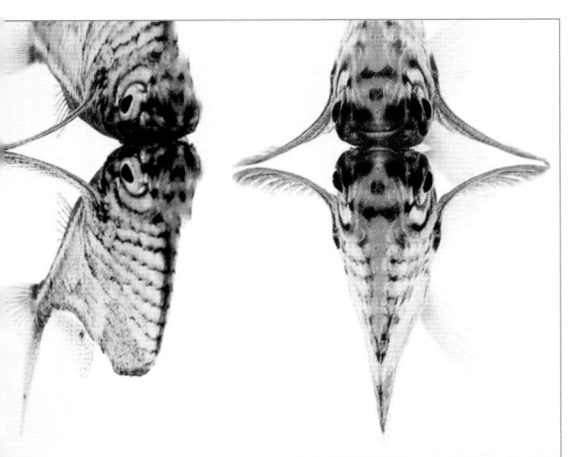

genera *Metynnis*, *Myleus* and *Mylossoma*, which eat nothing more controversial than fruit and soft-leaved plants.

Still in South America, tiny, surface-swimming hatchetfishes are ideal for community tanks. They have deep bodies and use their pectoral fins as wings to leap into the air to escape predators.

Pencilfishes are peaceful, slimline beauties that spend much of their time in midwater, often in a 'head-up' position. One of them, *Nannostomus eques*, has a bold lateral stripe extending into the lower tail lobe, explaining its common name of 'Hockey Stick

Tetra'. This feature is shared by the Penguin Tetra *(Thayeria boehlkei)*.

For bold patterning, it is hard to beat the Striped Headstander *(Anostomus anostomus)*, whose markings run from head-to-tail, or the Banded Leporinus *(Leporinus fasciatus)*, which seems to be wearing a black-and-yellow jersey.

Relatively few African characins come into the hobby, but the Congo Tetra *(Phenacogrammus interruptus)* is a noteworthy exception. For the larger aquarium there are two species of algae-grazing *Distichodus* species, with vertical barring as sharp and clear as on any Asian Clown Loach.

LONG-NOSED
DISTICHODUS

Distichodus lusosso

Mature size: *40cm (16in)*

Characteristics: *Most aquarium characins originate from South America, but this barred beauty is from Africa's Zaire Basin. The fatty adipose fin (behind the dorsal) is a characin trademark, although nobody is sure of its use, or even if it has one. In the wild, these fishes graze on algae growing on rocks, and a brightly lit aquarium will encourage a supply of this vegetarian fare. Note the adult size – these are not suitable for small or heavily planted tanks, whose décor they will uproot, and they can be aggressive towards smaller fishes.*

ROUND-FACED
DISTICHODUS

Distichodus sexfasciatus
Mature size: *100cm (39in)*
Characteristics: *A little Latin helps enormously in understanding your fishes; 'sexfasciatus' means six-banded. The underslung, hard-lipped mouth of this giant suggests specialized algae-grazing in rock crevices. The scales reach well into the wrist of the deeply forked tail. This species is reputed to be more peaceful than D. lusosso, and is an egg-scatterer, but has never been bred in home aquariums. There are no known external sexual differences.*

Long-nosed

Round-faced

CARDINAL TETRA

Paracheirodon axelrodi
Mature size: *4cm (1.6in)*
Characteristics: *They caused a stir when first imported into the USA in 1956, soon challenging Neons for the title of most popular tropical aquarium fish. Red belly, blue iridescent stripe, white-bordered dorsal and anal fins and prominent eyes, luminescent under artificial light and peaceful into the bargain – quite a combination! The bigger the shoal, the better the effect, especially against a dark background.*

NEON TETRA

Paracheirodon innesi
Mature size: *5cm (2in)*
Characteristics: *Nothing matches the sight of a large shoal of Neons darting through dense plant cover. They appear lit from within. Aquarium spawnings are not too difficult in soft, acidic water, provided the parents are removed and the tank is shaded for a week after the fry hatch. Females are the plumper sex. Mass production on fish farms has brought the price tumbling down, and Neons are now 'pocket money' purchases.*

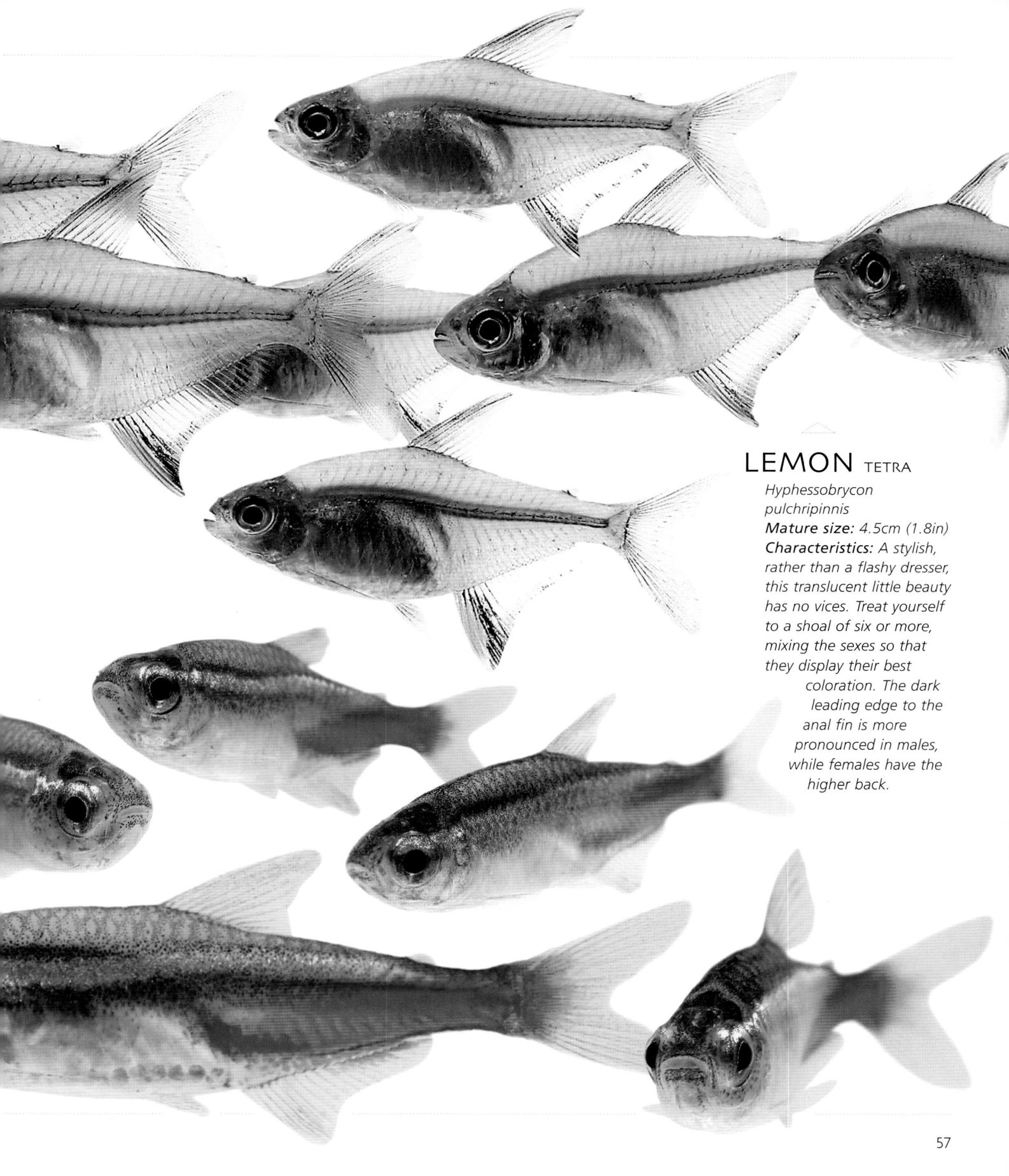

LEMON TETRA

*Hyphessobrycon
pulchripinnis*
Mature size: *4.5cm (1.8in)*
Characteristics: *A stylish,
rather than a flashy dresser,
this translucent little beauty
has no vices. Treat yourself
to a shoal of six or more,
mixing the sexes so that
they display their best
coloration. The dark
leading edge to the
anal fin is more
pronounced in males,
while females have the
higher back.*

RED PIRANHA

Serrasalmus nattereri
Mature size: *28cm (11in)*
Characteristics: *The reputation of this fish goes before it, and the morbid fascination factor is largely responsible for its popularity. The spotted youngsters will certainly nip and scrap among themselves, so that choosing a perfect specimen can be difficult. In maturity, the Red Piranha is something of an introvert (except at feeding time), and needs a well-furnished tank and the company of shoalmates. Aquarium spawnings are quite common, the fish scattering eggs among plants.*

A PREDATOR IN THE MAKING

The heavily muscled lower jaw and conical, razor-sharp teeth of the Piranha make the perfect 'dice-'n'-slice' machine, and fish or mammal prey can be stripped to the bone in short order. The teeth are clearly visible in these growing fish, which are still 'juvenile' at 8-12 months old. Preserved curio specimens have jaw tissue stripped away, exposing the teeth, but this is how they appear in living fishes. Live foods are not necessary in the aquarium, as Piranha will readily adapt to strips of lancefish, clams, prawns and other 'meaty' items.

RED HOOK

Myleus rubripinnis
Mature size: *15cm (6in)*
Characteristics: *Ideal fish for anyone wanting a drama-free 'piranha', these close relatives look the part but feed on plants and small invertebrates, rather than other fish. The common name refers to the coloration and shape of the anal fin. A stately shoal in a spacious, deep aquarium looks great as light mirrors off their flanks.*

SILVER DOLLAR

Metynnis argenteus
Mature size: *14cm (5.5in)*
Characteristics: *These aptly named characins from Brazil and Guyana lay up to 2,000 eggs amid floating plants. However, aquarium spawnings are rare, possibly because few people have the space to grow these fish to maturity. Despite their menacing stare (left), they are strictly vegetarian, so no plants, unless you want to give them an expensive snack.*

BLEEDING HEART TETRA

Hyphessobrycon erythrostigma
Mature size: *6cm (2.4in)*
Characteristics: *The red flank patch gives this Upper Amazonian fish its common name. Males have dorsal and anal fin extensions, making sexing of mature specimens easy.*
Aquarium stalwarts and deservedly popular.

GLOWLIGHT TETRA
Hemigrammus erythrozonus
Mature size: *4cm (1.6in)*
Characteristics: *These tiny fish appear to glow, leading newcomers to believe that they generate their own light. A convincing illusion, probably assisting shoals to stay close-knit in their sun-dappled Guyanan home waters.*

CONGO TETRA
Phenacogrammus interruptus
Mature size: *8cm (3.2in)*
Characteristics: *The males (here) sport elongated dorsal and caudal finnage, and both sexes have large, reflective scales that show best against a dark background and substrate. These active swimmers from Zaire require a large tank.*

SERPAE TETRA

Hyphessobrycon eques
Mature size: *4cm (1.6in)*
Characteristics: *Serpae tetras have been a popular choice for aquariums for many years and today these deep-bodied fishes from the Southern Amazon are commercially bred by the million. The black dorsal fin and flank flashes contrast well with the rich, coppery body through which the swimbladder can be seen to shine.*

PENGUIN TETRA ✳

Thayeria boehlkei
Mature size: *6cm (2.4in)*
Characteristics: *'Hockey Stick' is
another name for these dapper
little fish, which can produce up
to 1,000 eggs at every
spawning. Females are
deeper in the body than
males, and both sexes
tend to swim with the
head slightly raised.*

MARBLED
HATCHETFISH

*Carnegiella
strigata*
Mature size:
4cm (1.6in)
Characteristics:
*These deep-bodied
characins, lacking an
adipose fin, are
surface-dwellers
that appreciate
a strong current
and pure, soft
water. Eggs can just be seen developing
in the body of the female (top), while
males are more strikingly marked.*

♂

BANDED
LEPORINUS

Leporinus fasciatus
Mature size: *25cm (10in)*
Characteristics: *Do not give this
denizen of the Amazon tributaries
a planted home, as it will dine on
the décor. Although also called
'headstander', it usually swims on an
even keel, unlike another 'headstander',
the horizontally barred Anostomus
ternetzi. These fish prefer a cool tank.*

♀

Giving birth to live young is a much more efficient means of reproduction than either random egg-scattering or parental brood care, since the fishes come into the world fully formed and ready to fend for themselves.

LIVEBE

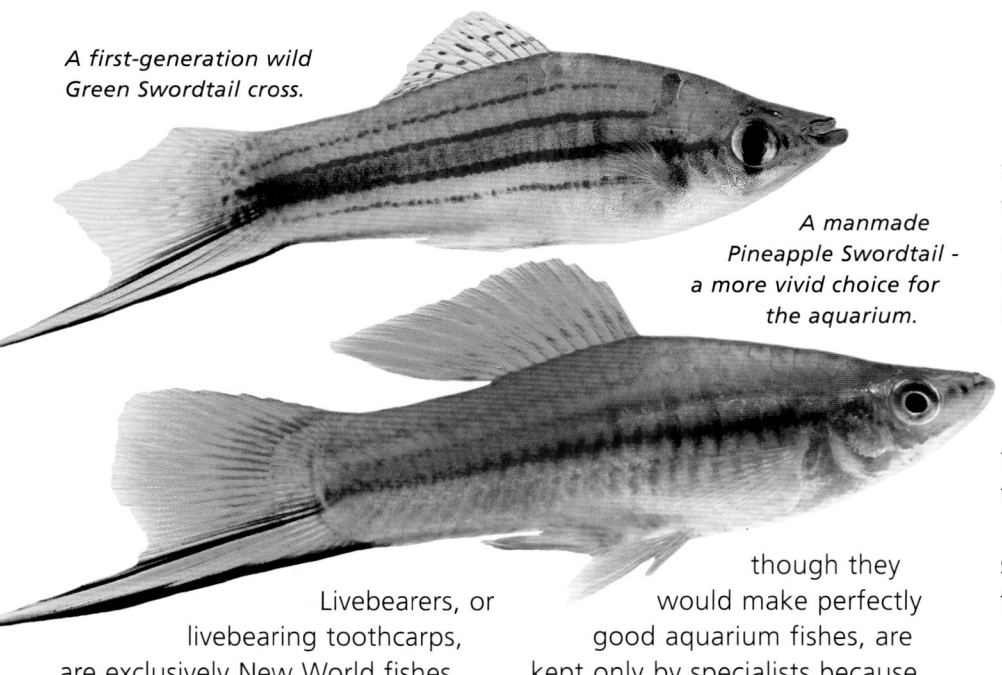

A first-generation wild Green Swordtail cross.

A manmade Pineapple Swordtail - a more vivid choice for the aquarium.

Livebearers perform internal fertilization, something they share with sharks, skates and rays. The males possess a gonopodium – a modified anal fin – with which to inseminate females. In all but the Goodeids, females can store sperm for months on end, and produce several broods without further male intervention. But in the aquarium this seldom happens.

Almost all livebearers seen for sale are commercially bred, and the farmed Guppy *(Poecilia reticulata)*

Livebearers, or livebearing toothcarps, are exclusively New World fishes, their natural range taking in the southern states of the USA, Central and parts of South America, and the Caribbean. However, some species (notably Mosquitofishes of the genus *Gambusia*) have been introduced around the world in the fight against malaria – by eating mosquito larvae at the surface.

Many livebearers have extremely localized habitats and are endangered in the wild; others, though they would make perfectly good aquarium fishes, are kept only by specialists because they are not particularly exciting to look at. The hobby is dominated by the family Poeciliidae, of which the genera *Poecilia* (Guppies and Mollies) and *Xiphophorus* (Platies and Swordtails) are far and away the best represented.

Fan-dancer. A Green Sailfin Molly preens before his mate.

is a world away from the wild Mexican population. Selective breeding continues to 'improve' on nature, with wildly extravagant tail and dorsal finnage and every imaginable coloration readily available. However, it is hard to improve upon the wild Green Sailfin Molly *(Poecilia velifera)*, from Mexico and Yucatan – all breeders have done is to cultivate the albino, or golden, form.

Platies *(Xiphophorus maculatus)* are produced in hi-fin varieties, but most retain their original sturdy body shape and short finnage, and it is only the coloration that has been experimented with. Commercial 'Variatus' platies probably carry Swordtail blood, as crosses with *Xiphophorus helleri* are quite viable.

To breed Platies, Guppies or Swords true to their ornamental strain, you need fishes of proven lineage and 'virgin'

These Balloon Mollies are not obese, they are just bred to look this way.

Guppies readily take insect and other prepared foods from the water surface.

females: this can be difficult, as they can be sexually mature within a matter of weeks. Most fishkeepers are happy just to see successive broods produced, and a self-perpetuating livebearer population of 'mongrels'.

NEON BLUE
GUPPY

Poecilia reticulata
Mature size: *6cm (2.4in)*
Characteristics: *The fish featured here are all delta-tailed male guppies. The various strains, bearing exotic trade names such as Neon Blue, Snakeskin, Green Lace, Golden, King Cobra, Half-black or Disco, may breed true if kept apart. But most hobbyists are content with a mixture; seeing how the young turn out only adds to the excitement. Pregnant females show a dark gravid spot on the abdomen.*

KING COBRA GUPPY

Poecilia reticulata
Mature size: *6cm (2.4in)*
Characteristics: *Unlike their drab wild ancestors, farmed guppies are available in almost limitless permutations of coloration and fin shape. Selective breeding has given the males exaggerated, flowing tails, used in continual courtship displays. The plainer, more rotund females are impregnated by the modified anal fin (gonopodium) of their suitors, and give birth to up to 40 live young.*

GOLDEN GUPPY

Poecilia reticulata
Mature size: *6cm (2.4in)*
Characteristics: *Guppies
are originally from
Central America, but
will be happy in a wide
temperature band
(18-28°C/64-82°F), given
hard, neutral water.
Avoid keeping them with
boisterous barbs or male
Siamese Fighters of the
same coloration, which
may mistake guppies for
rivals and attack them.*

GREEN SAILFIN MOLLY

Poecilia velifera

Mature size: 18cm (7in)

Characteristics: Both the wild-caught fish from Mexico and Yucatan and a cross between Poecilia velifera and P. latipinna *bear the same common name. Both need plenty of green food and, given the male's amazing but vulnerable dorsal fin, these fish do best in a species, rather than a community, tank. They prefer hard water to which some marine salt has been added.*

♀

ORANGE SAILFIN MOLLY

Poecilia velifera
Mature size: *18cm (7in)*
Characteristics: *This farm-bred albino version of the Green Sailfin Molly lacks all the dark pigment. The sailfin characteristics are exaggerated in this fish. Note the gonopodiums in the two males shown below.*

SILVER SAILFIN MOLLY

Poecilia spp.
Mature size: *18cm (7in)*
Characteristics: *This cross between the two most common Molly species shows a lyre tail and a moderately tall dorsal fin. The more extreme Silver Balloon Molly has a deep, foreshortened body.*

♂

BLUE ONE-SPOT
PLATY

Xiphophorus maculatus
Mature size: *6cm (2.4in)*
Characteristics: *In these livebearers, there are countless variations of coloration and finnage over the original Mexican ancestor. Sexes are easily told apart by the anal fin; in the male it has become modified into an internal organ of fertilization known as a gonopodium.*

Male   Female

♂

♀

ORANGE PLATY

Xiphophorus maculatus
Mature size: *6cm (2.4in)*
Characteristics: *In the best examples of these peaceable fishes, the startlingly vivid body coloration is carried through into all the fins. These are males.*

RED WAGTAIL PLATY

Xiphophorus maculatus
Mature size: 6cm (2.4in)
Characteristics: With fin rays picked
out in black, and a uniform crimson
body, these livebearers (here males) are
the ultimate in everyday aquarium chic.

TUXEDO PLATY

Xiphophorus maculatus
Mature size: 6cm (2.4in)
Characteristics: In their smart
but understated formal livery,
these Platies are a good foil to
examples with more showy
coloration. Be aware that all
strains readily interbreed, so
try to keep them separate.
These are females.

PINEAPPLE
SWORDTAIL

Xiphophorus helleri
Mature size: *10cm (4in)*
Characteristics:
The wild fish, from Central America, is an unexceptional green, but the breeders have got to work to produce several striking varieties. Males have the long, swordlike extension to the lower lobe of the tail fin, but this comes only with time. The females are larger and more thickset.

BLACK SWORDTAIL

Xiphophorus helleri
Mature size: *10cm (4in)*
Characteristics: *This is the Swordtail version of the closely related Tuxedo Platy, and interbreeding of the two species is suspected.*

GREEN STRIPED
SWORDTAIL

Xiphophorus helleri
Mature size: *10cm (4in)*
Characteristics: *Pregnant females show what is known as a gravid spot, which is visible in the fish at top. Apparently stunted swordtail males are often the most fertile, and will beat their larger tankmates in the pursuit of a suitable mate.*

♂

♀

RED WAG SWORDTAIL

Xiphophorus helleri
Mature size: *10cm (4in)*
Characteristics: *These fishes are always actively chasing one another. Among livebearers, sex really does make the world go round!*

♀

♂

Fish eggs through the mail? That is how some enthusiasts increase their stocks of these incandescent little fishes, whose lives flame all too briefly.

While killifishes are not mainstream in the hobby, they are fascinating to keep, and ideal for anyone without the space to run a full-scale aquarium. Most species can be housed and bred in small tanks. Properly known as egglaying toothcarps, they are widely distributed across Africa, Asia and the Americas. Their closest relatives are the familiar livebearers such as guppies and platies, but, because of the often hostile nature of their environment, some have developed ingenious breeding strategies to ensure survival through the generations.

To get the best from killifish, you should try to spawn them, if only to maintain stocks. Those from savannah regions, for example, inhabit ponds that dry up every year. Before that happens, and the parent fishes die, tough eggs are deposited, like tiny time capsules, into the bottom mud. These hatch when the rains return. These killies are known as 'annuals' and,

Aphyosemion gardneri nigerianum – a popular killie among hobbyists.

although they may survive beyond a year in the aquarium, they are, by definition, short-lived. Yet their beauty is unrivalled, the males with their large dorsal and anal fins, the tail often lyre-shaped, and the whole body suffused with spangled patterns of almost unreal brightness. The West African genus *Aphyosemion* is the most popular of all.

Once their eggs are laid, collect and store them in damp peat in a warm, dark place for the incubation period, which can be several months. Then, add water from an established killie tank and the fry will hatch in hours. With

time short to attain maturity, they grow fast, and need copious amounts of small, live food items.

Killifish from more stable habitats lay their eggs on the roots of floating plants, but in the hobby a spawning mop is substituted.

SHES

Like other killifishes, this male Aphyosemion walkeri is more showy than the female.

Killies are small, but beautifully marked. Tail design varies among males, but all are aimed at attracting mates.

The flowing fins and bold markings of the Cape Lopez Lyretail (Aphyosemion australe).

Eggs can be picked off this, or left in place and stored in a jar of tank water, where they will hatch in two to three weeks. Typical plant-spawners are killies of the genus *Epiplatys* (commonly known as Panchax), from West Africa. They look like miniature pike, and need to be kept in a species tank or with larger tankmates, as they are predatory.

One of the best-known killifish, the American flagfish *(Jordanella floridae)*, from Florida, is often not recognized as such, because it looks like a platy and its reproductive behaviour is more akin to that of a cichlid, with the male caring for the brood. Killies are full of surprises.

APHYOSEMION
GARDNERI

Gardner's Aphyosemion
Mature size: 6cm (2.4in)
*Characteristics: This is a yellow variety –
others are blue. Males (here) are brighter,
while females of the various subspecies
all look much alike and are a
pale tan. These fish
fare best in a
shaded species tank,
and are known as
'substrate-spawners',
laying their eggs in bottom
detritus. A ratio of three
females to each male
brings the best chance
of spawning
success.*

APHYOSEMION OGOENSE
PYROPHORE

Mature size: 5cm (2in)
*Characteristics: The candy-striped fins and lyre tail
of the male make this a sought-after, though
rather rare, West African killie. After a courtship of
much chasing and display, adhesive eggs are laid
on plants or, in the aquarium, a spawning mop.
Note the large eyes, set well up the head – typical
of a fish that is both predator and prey.*

♂

♀

♀

♂

APHYOSEMION GARDNERI
NIGERIANUM

Steel-blue Lyretail
Mature size: *6cm (2.4in)*
Characteristics: *Their common name does not do
these little gems justice – any artist painting them
as nature has done would be accused of letting
their imagination run riot. They rival any cultivated
guppy, yet these are wild fishes from Nigeria.*

♀

SCRIPTAPHYOSEMION
RIGGENBACHI 'DIBENG GOLD'

Mature size: 10cm (4in)
Characteristics: This fish typifies the appeal of African annual killies – tiny stars of the fish world that burn all too briefly before the sun's heat dries their home pools and they die. These are peaceful fishes that will live in a community aquarium, provided their tankmates are no larger, otherwise the extravagant fins of these male fish could become a target.

♂

EPIPLATYS
CHAPERI ANGONA

Mature size: 6.5cm (2.5in)
Characteristics: New subspecies of Epiplatys chaperi *from West Africa continue to come into the hobby. In this pair, the difference between the sexes in terms of size and coloration is clearly illustrated. The glory of the male lies not so much in its subtle body livery as in its large, orange pectoral fins, compared to those of the female, which are clear.*

EPIPLATYS ROLOFFI

Roloff's Panchax
Mature size: 7cm (2.75in)
Characteristics: Like all panchax, these West African fishes have large mouths suited to taking insect prey from the surface, where they spend much of their time. They lay adhesive eggs on plants and so can be bred on spawning mops. The blue head of the males (below) makes a superb contrast with the reticulated scales and rainbow-edged finnage.

♀

♂

PACHYPANCHAX
SAKARAMYI

Mature size: *7cm (2.75in)*
Characteristics: *This relatively subdued killie from Madagascar can live in quite brackish water, and lays adhesive eggs on plants. The smaller female is translucent, the skeletal structure showing clearly through the skin.*

♀

♂

JORDANELLA FLORIDAE

American Flagfish

Mature size: *6cm (2.4in)*
Characteristics: *The stars and stripes are prominent on this hugely popular aquarium fish, whose stocky body is not typical of killies. The slightly smaller and less vivid female has a dark spot to the rear of the dorsal fin. Her mate gets the good parenting award for brood care.*

FUNDULOPANCHAX
SPOORENBERGI

Spoorenberg's Panchax
Mature size: *12cm (4.7in)*

Characteristics: *These substrate-divers grow to a good size (for killies). The yellow-edged tails and fins of these males almost glow, and are shown to best effect when they are displaying to potential mates. Killifish prefer soft, neutral water, but will survive in less suitable tank environments, too.*

We can SCUBA dive in a watery world. Anabantids turn the tables, breathing air at the surface. That's not the only remarkable thing about these complex, fascinating fishes.

ANABA

Coping with potentially hostile environments is a major key to success in the fish world, and the labyrinth fishes (popularly known as anabantids) have evolved physical characteristics and breeding techniques that place them high in the survival stakes. The suborder to which they belong, Anabantoidei, includes five families, but only the family Belontidae (Gouramis, Siamese Fighting Fish, Combtails and Paradisefish) is well represented in the fishkeeping hobby. Most of these fishes are small, vivid, well-behaved, and relatively easy to keep and breed. Anabantids come from Africa and Asia; most hobby fish are imported from the Far East.

The 'labyrinth' is a respiratory organ located above each gill chamber, enabling anabantids to breathe atmospheric oxygen. Air is gulped in at the surface and forced into the labyrinth, which is furnished with a rich capillary blood supply. Oxygen diffuses into the bloodstream and carbon dioxide is unloaded before the spent air is expelled through the

Threadlike pelvic fins act as a personal navigation and food-finding system.

Anabantids gulp surface air to fill their labyrinth organs. These spongy outgrowths of the gill chamber act like 'lungs' to boost oxygen levels in the blood. By contrast, these fishes blow bubbles during nest building.

gills. As a result, these fishes can inhabit roadside ditches and rice paddies, whose oxygen-deficient and often polluted waters would prove fatal to most others. Some gouramis even have greatly extended, threadlike pelvic fins to 'feel' their way through the murk and find food (small aquatic insects and crustaceans). The two modes of breathing complement one another, so that if an anabantid is unable to visit the surface at regular intervals, it will die. The other characteristic survival technique relates to breeding. Bubblenesting, with male parental care, gives fry a good chance of avoiding predation in the critical first days of life, and therefore broods are typically smaller than those of egg-scatterers. Bubblenests are constructed by the males, and vary in size and complexity according to species. Some incorporate plant matter, others rely purely on a film of saliva around each bubble to hold them together. On completion of the nest, the pair entwine below it in a spawning embrace, where eggs are released and fertilized.

A male Siamese Fighting Fish spreads his fins to challenge a rival head-on.

These are gathered by the male, who spits them into their blanket of bubbles and guards them until they hatch. In gouramis of the genus *Trichogaster* the eggs float, but in the Siamese Fighting Fish *(Betta splendens)* they sink,

and the male is kept busy returning them to the nest. Newly hatched fry take an initial gulp of surface air to fill their swimbladders. This air is warm and humid in the wild, and so for successful aquarium spawnings keep the tank covered.

SIAMESE
FIGHTING FISH

Betta splendens
Mature size: 7cm (2.75in)
Characteristics: Devoted parent but merciless to other males, the male Siamese Fighter lives its short life on the edge. Flowing fins and flared gill covers (below) are displayed as threat gestures that quickly develop into ferocious attacks on each other's fins. A sole male will live peacefully in a community aquarium, but a breeding pair need a well-planted tank to themselves. Even then, the testosterone-fuelled male can turn on his plainer mate. As in other bubblenesters, the male guards the eggs floating at the surface. Selective breeding has produced ever-more extravagant finnage in shimmering combinations of red, blue, green and gold.

SIAMESE
FIGHTING FISH

Betta splendens
Mature size: 7cm (2.75in)
Characteristics: In repose, this male steel-blue Betta shows off his beautiful trailing finnage, which is far more elaborate than would be found in the wild fish. How long will he be around to flaunt his finery? In an aquarium, even without the presence of a female and the pressures of fatherhood to keep him running on adrenalin, two years is a good age for a Siamese Fighter. His life is high-octane but short, so treat him well. Do not mix him with fin-nippers, or taunt him with rival males in nearby tanks, otherwise he will conduct his aggression dramas through the glass and burn out like the fiery living candle he is.

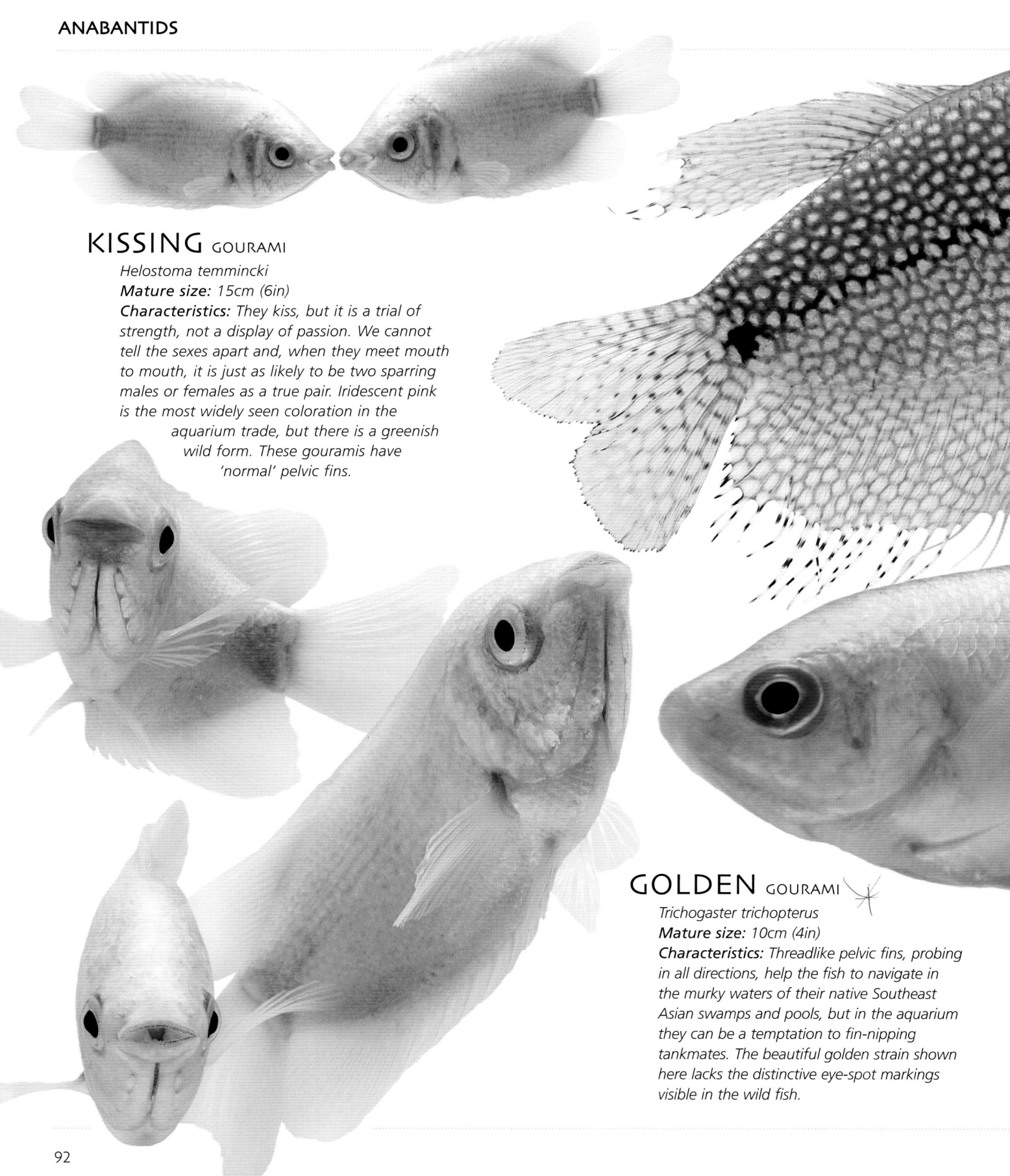

KISSING GOURAMI

Helostoma temmincki
Mature size: *15cm (6in)*
Characteristics: *They kiss, but it is a trial of strength, not a display of passion. We cannot tell the sexes apart and, when they meet mouth to mouth, it is just as likely to be two sparring males or females as a true pair. Iridescent pink is the most widely seen coloration in the aquarium trade, but there is a greenish wild form. These gouramis have 'normal' pelvic fins.*

GOLDEN GOURAMI

Trichogaster trichopterus
Mature size: *10cm (4in)*
Characteristics: *Threadlike pelvic fins, probing in all directions, help the fish to navigate in the murky waters of their native Southeast Asian swamps and pools, but in the aquarium they can be a temptation to fin-nipping tankmates. The beautiful golden strain shown here lacks the distinctive eye-spot markings visible in the wild fish.*

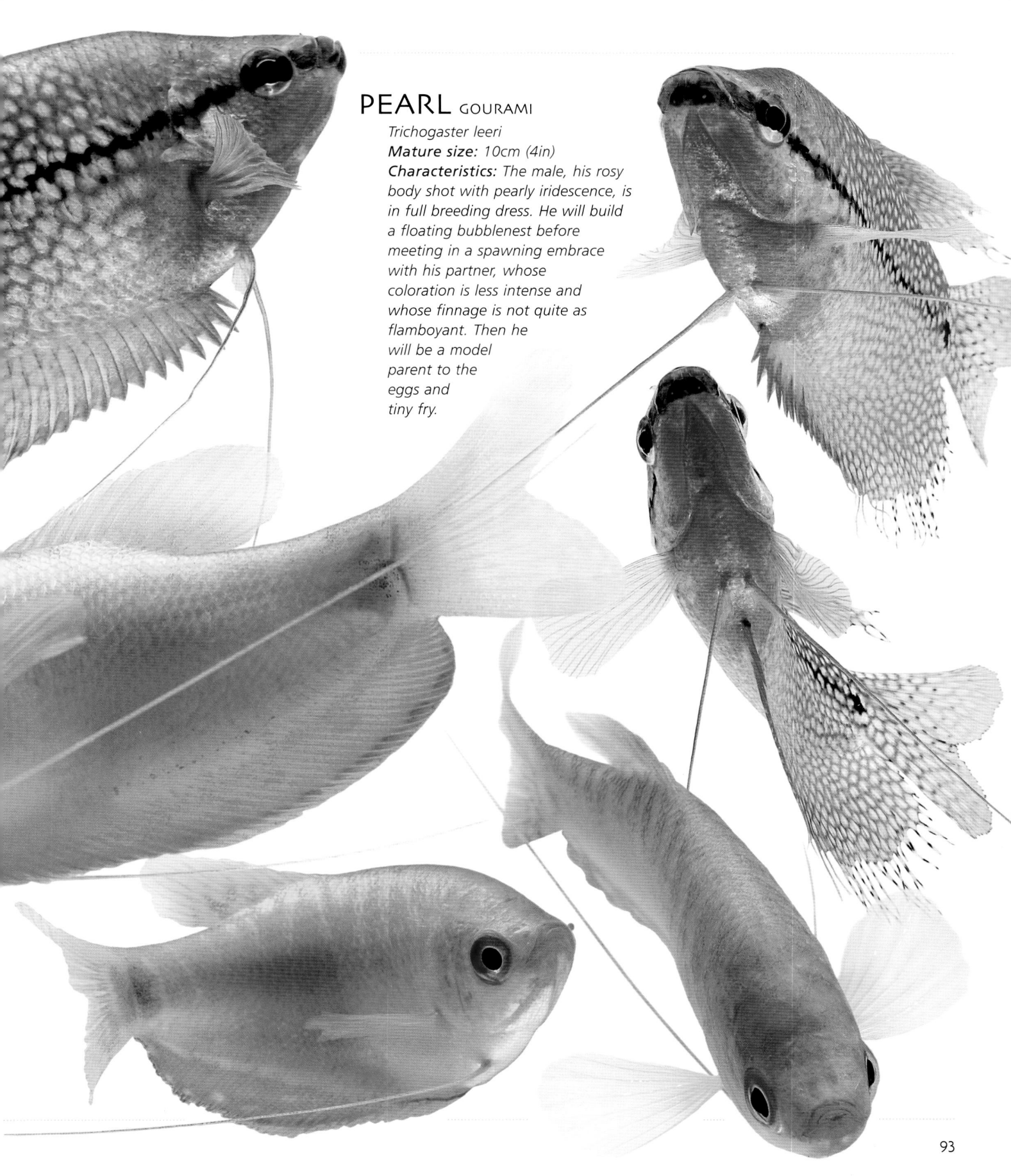

PEARL GOURAMI

Trichogaster leeri
Mature size: 10cm (4in)
Characteristics: The male, his rosy body shot with pearly iridescence, is in full breeding dress. He will build a floating bubblenest before meeting in a spawning embrace with his partner, whose coloration is less intense and whose finnage is not quite as flamboyant. Then he will be a model parent to the eggs and tiny fry.

ROYAL RED
GOURAMI

Colisa lalia

Mature size: 5cm (2in)

Characteristics: Two species on this page are aquarium variants of the Dwarf Gourami, in which the males show vertical flank barring and blue-and-red spangling on the body and fins, while females are plainer and more silvery. In the Royal Red, only the more pointed dorsal of the male is a sure way of identifying the sexes. The humped shoulder profile is typical of Dwarf Gouramis. They are peaceable, if somewhat shy.

♂

♀

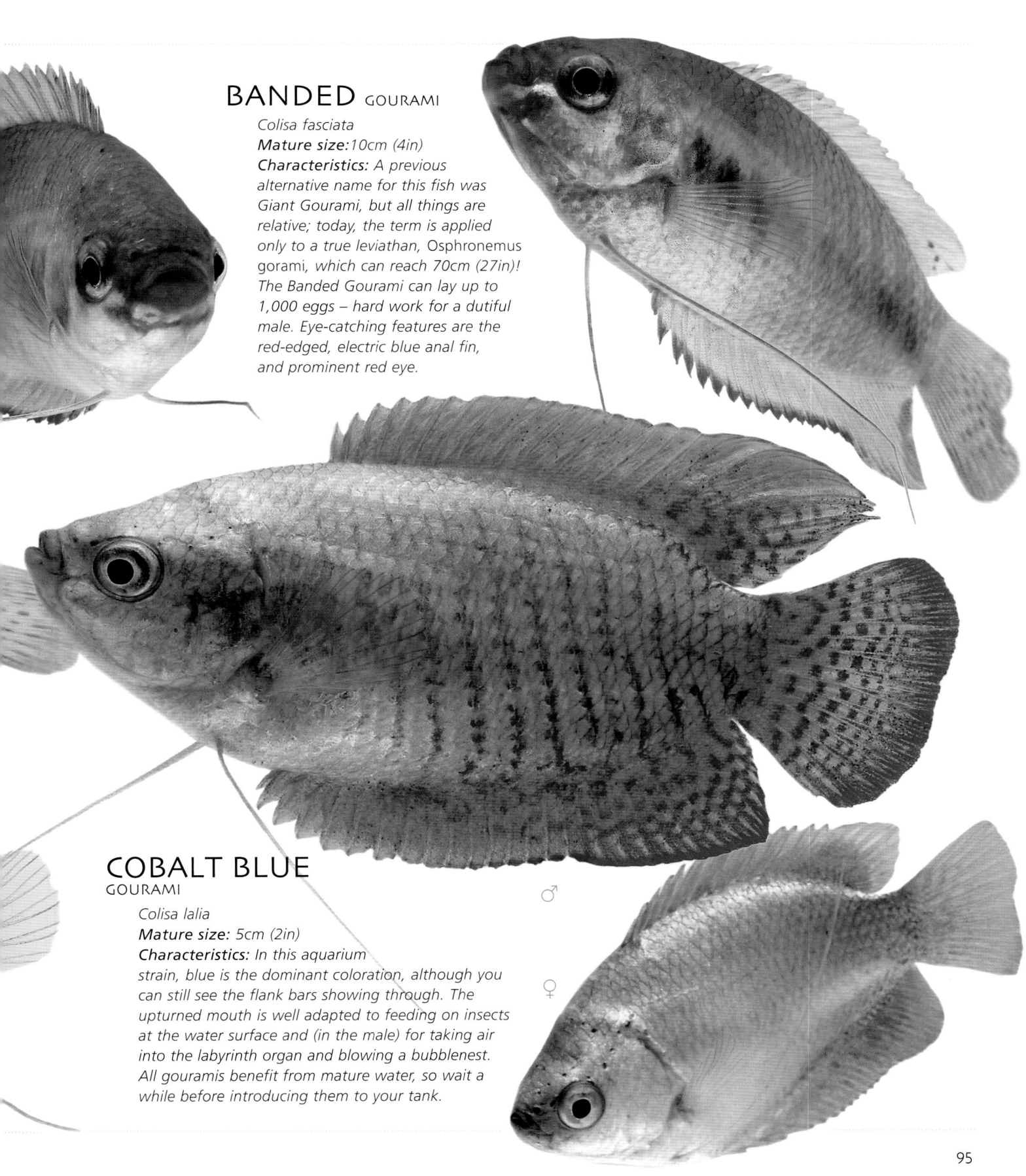

BANDED GOURAMI

Colisa fasciata
Mature size: 10cm (4in)
Characteristics: A previous
alternative name for this fish was
Giant Gourami, but all things are
relative; today, the term is applied
only to a true leviathan, Osphronemus
gorami, which can reach 70cm (27in)!
The Banded Gourami can lay up to
1,000 eggs – hard work for a dutiful
male. Eye-catching features are the
red-edged, electric blue anal fin,
and prominent red eye.

COBALT BLUE
GOURAMI

Colisa lalia
Mature size: 5cm (2in)
Characteristics: In this aquarium
strain, blue is the dominant coloration, although you
can still see the flank bars showing through. The
upturned mouth is well adapted to feeding on insects
at the water surface and (in the male) for taking air
into the labyrinth organ and blowing a bubblenest.
All gouramis benefit from mature water, so wait a
while before introducing them to your tank.

♂

♀

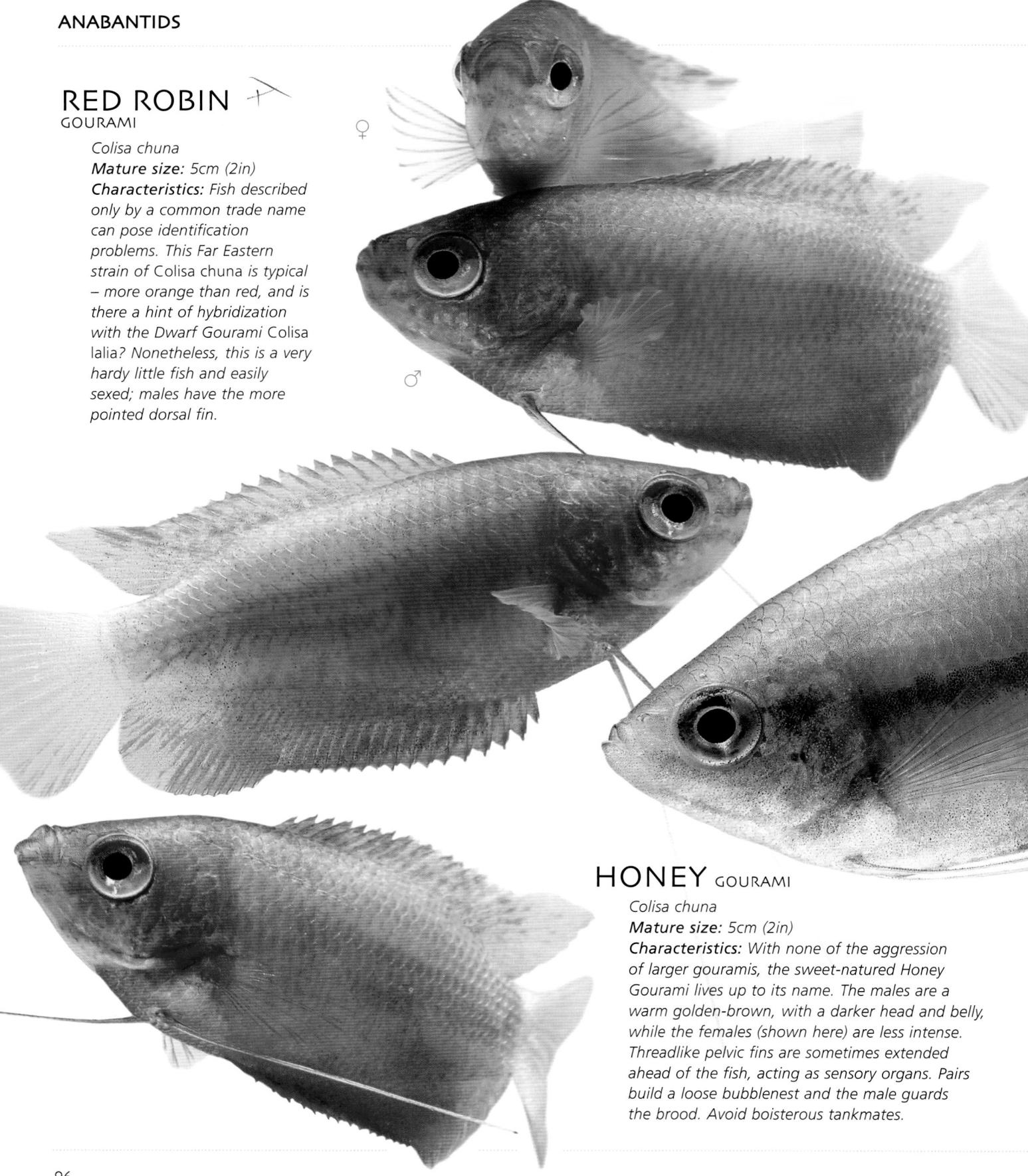

RED ROBIN
GOURAMI

Colisa chuna
Mature size: *5cm (2in)*
Characteristics: *Fish described only by a common trade name can pose identification problems. This Far Eastern strain of Colisa chuna is typical – more orange than red, and is there a hint of hybridization with the Dwarf Gourami Colisa lalia? Nonetheless, this is a very hardy little fish and easily sexed; males have the more pointed dorsal fin.*

♀

♂

HONEY GOURAMI

Colisa chuna
Mature size: *5cm (2in)*
Characteristics: *With none of the aggression of larger gouramis, the sweet-natured Honey Gourami lives up to its name. The males are a warm golden-brown, with a darker head and belly, while the females (shown here) are less intense. Threadlike pelvic fins are sometimes extended ahead of the fish, acting as sensory organs. Pairs build a loose bubblenest and the male guards the brood. Avoid boisterous tankmates.*

OPALINE GOURAMI

Trichogaster trichopterus

Mature size: *10cm (4in)*

Characteristics: *The wild fish, also known as the Three-spot Gourami, is mottled blue, with two black spots along the body (the eye being the third spot). Aquarium strains such as this result from crosses with Trichogaster trichopterus trichopterus, which grows slightly larger. Females become noticeably plump when ready to spawn. These gouramis are quite peaceful, although the occasional 'rogue' male can harass smaller tankmates.*

The beauty and grace of these inexpensive shoaling fishes lights up any community aquarium. The group includes some readily spawned species.

DANIOS, & RASBORAS

The Scissortail Rasbora scores highly in the small-fish popularity stakes.

Sooner or later, most aquarists like to increase their stocks by breeding their own fishes. Enter on cue the Zebra Danio *(Brachydanio rerio)*, the perfect egglayer for beginners. This little fish from India is easy to sex (females are more vivid, males slimmer), comes readily into condition, and will spawn virtually to order. I remember the first time I saw a pinstriped pair placed into a small breeding tank, bare except for a layer of glass marbles on the bottom. A measure of cold water dropped the temperature a couple of degrees and almost instantly the fishes began a whirling courtship dance, too fast for the eye to follow. Tiny, clear fertilized eggs fell into the crevices between the marbles, the

parents were removed, and a couple of days later the first fry were seen clinging, like tiny glass splinters, to the walls of the tank.

The only other egglayer remotely as obliging is the White Cloud Mountain Minnow *(Tanichthys albonubes)*, a small, cool water-loving cyprinid originally from China.

'Danio' describes fishes of two genera, *Brachydanio* and *Danio*, the difference being that *Brachydanio* has an incomplete lateral line (the sensory organ along the flanks). From a fishkeeping viewpoint, they can all be treated the same. All danios are from Southeast Asia, and are

Lively Gold Danios lack the blue pigment of their Zebra forebears.

MINNOWS

members of the carp family, Cyprinidae. They are streamlined, fast-swimming shoaling fishes that occupy the often under-populated middle layers of the aquarium. They pose no problems to tankmates and are agile enough to evade casual harassment.

The Zebra Danio is among the least expensive of tropical fishes, extensively farmed, with long-finned variants common. The Pearl Danio (Brachydanio albolineatus) is a slightly larger fish with an iridescent sheen. The Leopard Danio (Brachydanio frankei) is rather a mystery – some consider it a distinct species, others a sport of the Zebra Danio. The gold body is dappled with blue, a pattern that runs into the anal and caudal fins.

Two species of true Danio are suited to larger, planted aquariums. The Giant (Danio aequipinnatus) and Bengal Danio (Danio devario) are both fishes of running, rather than stagnant, water and require good aeration.

Rasboras are less easy to breed than danios, but otherwise are very similar in disposition. They are found from East Africa across eastern Asia to the Philippines and Indonesia. Harlequin, Clown and Scissortail Rasboras are justifiably popular aquarium fish. To encourage spawning, the water needs to be soft and acidic. Adults adapt to tapwater close to neutral.

A plump female Harlequin (Rasbora heteromorpha). In males, the vertical edge of the dark marking is sloping.

Spot the link – just join the dots and a Leopard Danio (top) becomes a Zebra. The two are clearly closely linked.

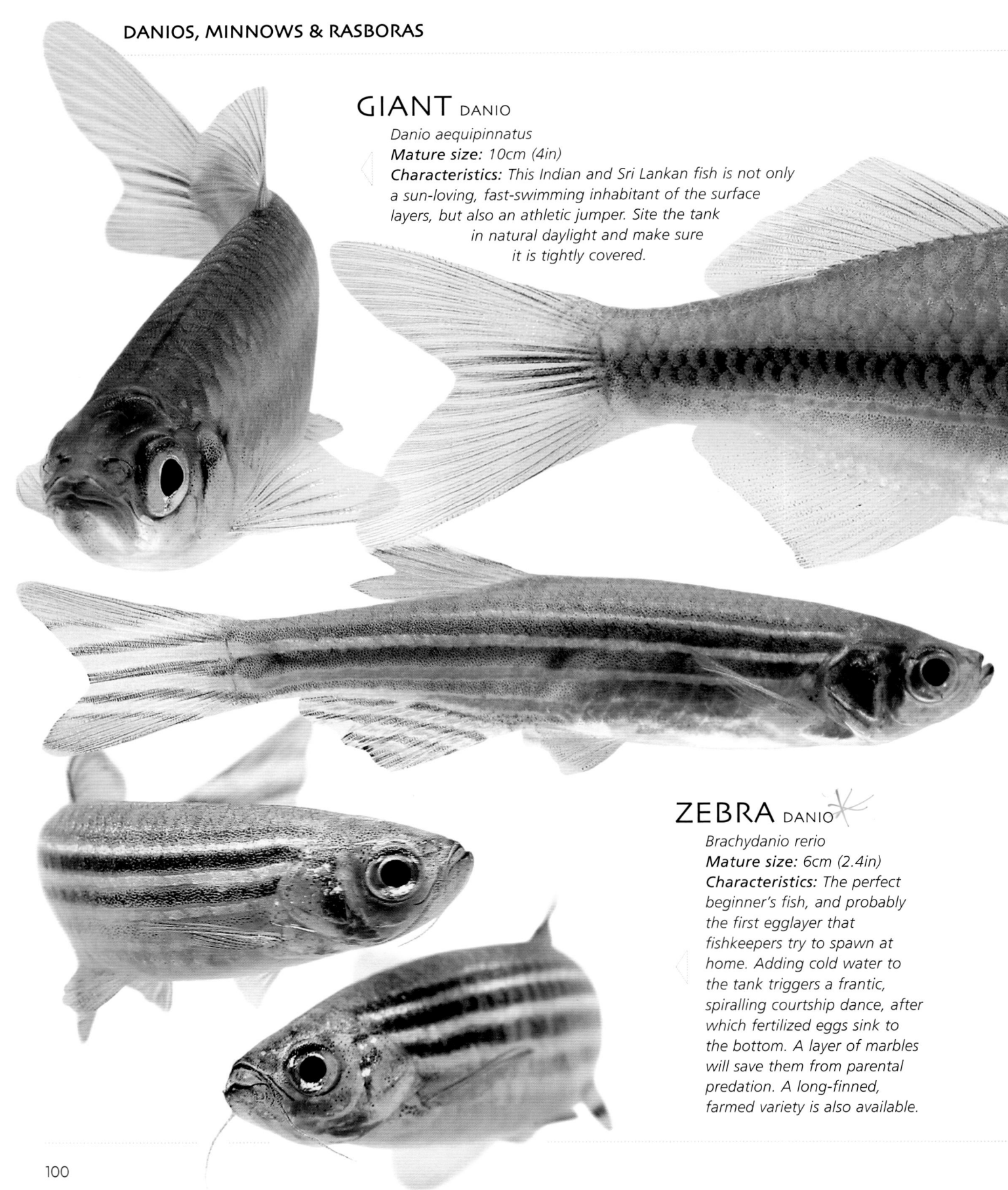

GIANT DANIO

Danio aequipinnatus
Mature size: *10cm (4in)*
Characteristics: *This Indian and Sri Lankan fish is not only a sun-loving, fast-swimming inhabitant of the surface layers, but also an athletic jumper. Site the tank in natural daylight and make sure it is tightly covered.*

ZEBRA DANIO

Brachydanio rerio
Mature size: *6cm (2.4in)*
Characteristics: *The perfect beginner's fish, and probably the first egglayer that fishkeepers try to spawn at home. Adding cold water to the tank triggers a frantic, spiralling courtship dance, after which fertilized eggs sink to the bottom. A layer of marbles will save them from parental predation. A long-finned, farmed variety is also available.*

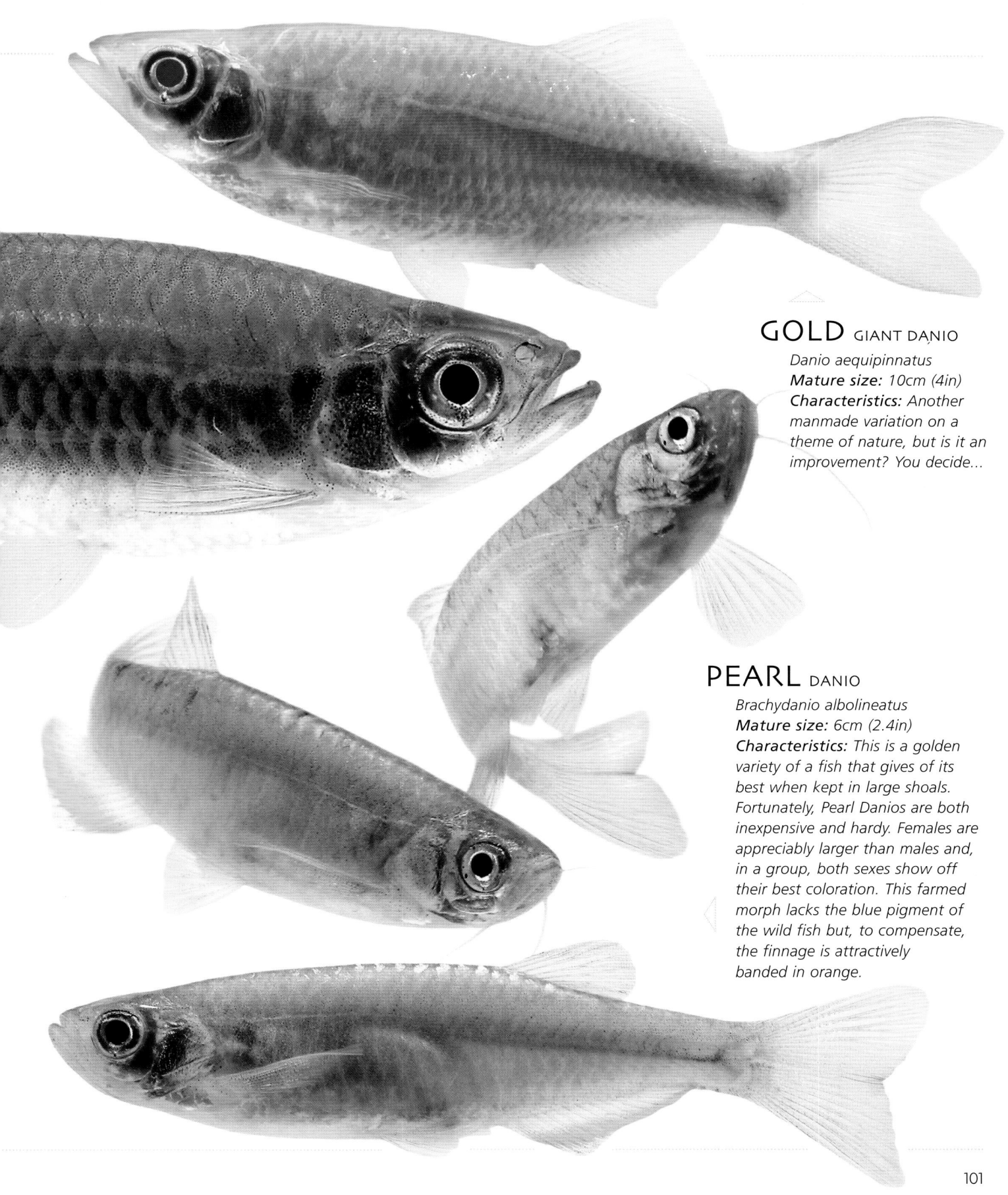

GOLD GIANT DANIO

Danio aequipinnatus
Mature size: *10cm (4in)*
Characteristics: *Another manmade variation on a theme of nature, but is it an improvement? You decide...*

PEARL DANIO

Brachydanio albolineatus
Mature size: *6cm (2.4in)*
Characteristics: *This is a golden variety of a fish that gives of its best when kept in large shoals. Fortunately, Pearl Danios are both inexpensive and hardy. Females are appreciably larger than males and, in a group, both sexes show off their best coloration. This farmed morph lacks the blue pigment of the wild fish but, to compensate, the finnage is attractively banded in orange.*

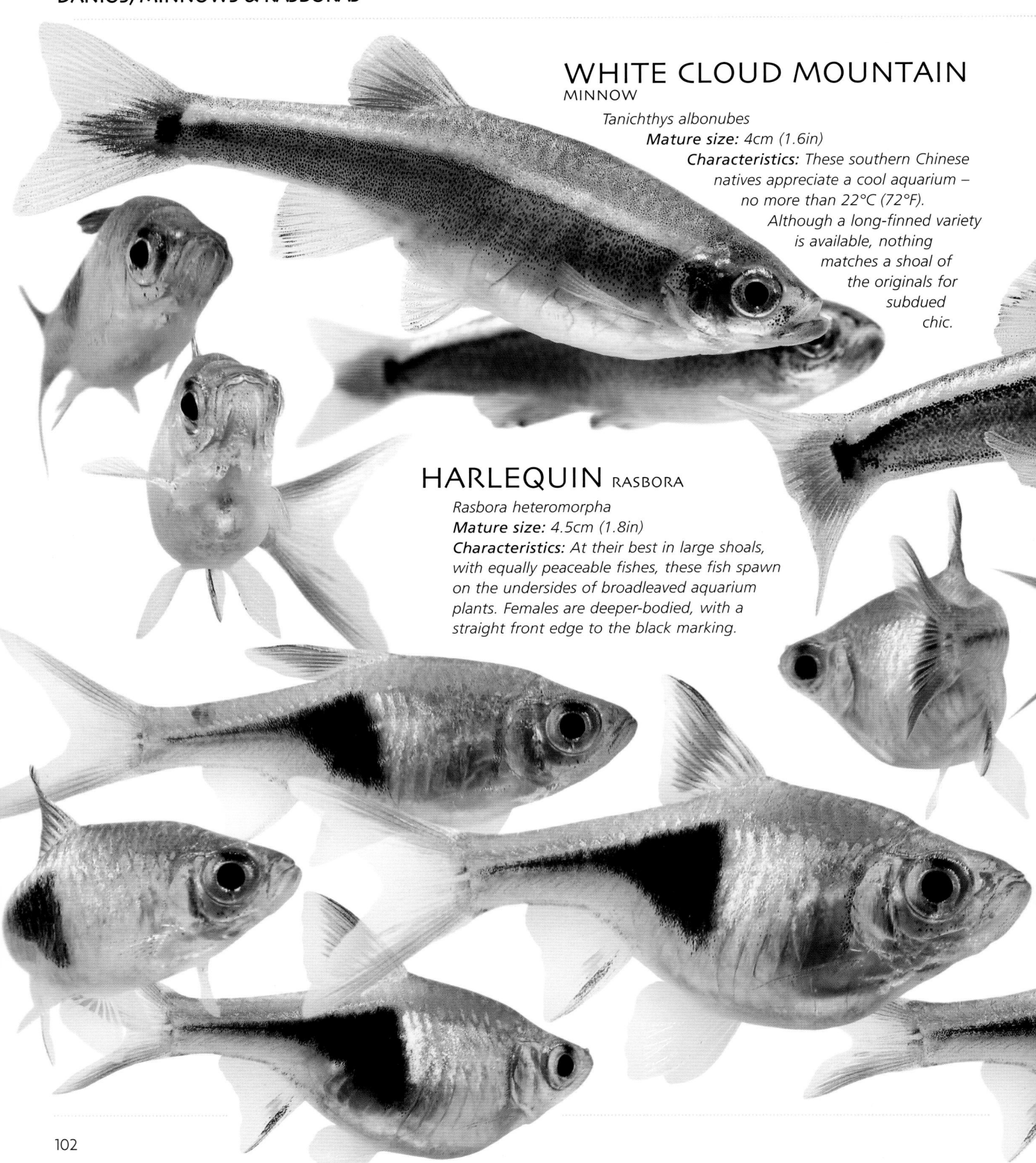

WHITE CLOUD MOUNTAIN
MINNOW

Tanichthys albonubes
Mature size: *4cm (1.6in)*
Characteristics: *These southern Chinese
natives appreciate a cool aquarium –
no more than 22°C (72°F).
Although a long-finned variety
is available, nothing
matches a shoal of
the originals for
subdued
chic.*

HARLEQUIN RASBORA

Rasbora heteromorpha
Mature size: *4.5cm (1.8in)*
Characteristics: *At their best in large shoals,
with equally peaceable fishes, these fish spawn
on the undersides of broadleaved aquarium
plants. Females are deeper-bodied, with a
straight front edge to the black marking.*

♀

♂

♀

♂

SCISSORTAIL RASBORA

Rasbora trilineatus
Mature size: *15cm (6in)*
Characteristics: *One of the larger rasboras, also known as 'Three-lined', these fishes hail from Malaysia, Sumatra and Borneo. Are those prominent tail markings a means of escaping predators with minimal collateral damage? That is where the eye of a piscivore would be drawn to.*

CATFIS

Catfishes are incredibly diverse and wide-ranging. It is hard to believe that an inoffensive, 5cm (2in) algae-eater from Brazil belongs to the same group as the glassy-eyed, fearsome 1.5m (5ft) predator *Hemibagrus wyckii* from Southeast Asia, whose velvet-black skin matches its dark disposition. And yet, when you realize that catfishes have successfully colonized all the tropical and temperate regions, it is clear that they have had to become masters of habitat exploitation.

What is a catfish? There are 34 catfish families, including marine and brackish water species, and common to them all is a lack of scales. Either their skins are naked or they are furnished with bony plates. Usually, but not always, it is the smaller prey catfish that are protected in this way. Catfishes are so named because they have 'whiskers', although in some species these are inconspicuous. These nerve-rich, paired sensory organs – known as barbels – are used to locate food and, in murky waters, for navigation. In some bagrids and pimelodids, they can be extravagantly long, sweeping almost the length of the body. In *Corydoras* catfishes, they are relatively short, while the

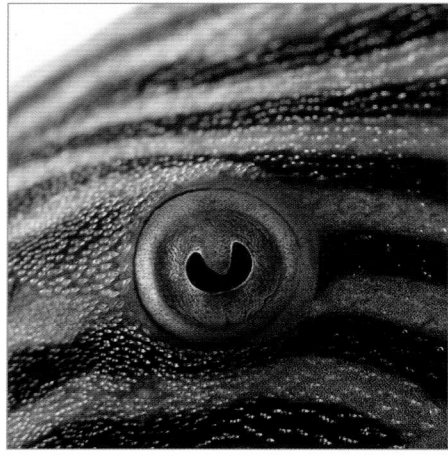

The omega eye in the Royal Plec (Panaque nigrolineatus) shades the sensitive retina from bright sunlight.

Corydoras (here C. gossei) are mistakenly imagined to be the scavengers among catfishes.

HES

bristlenose cats have only one pair of true barbels at the corners of their mouths, supplemented by fleshy outgrowths that are more prominent in the males.

Quirky lifestyles endear cats to fishkeepers. The African *Synodontis nigriventris* routinely swims upside-down – hence its common name of Upside-down Catfish – while its relative *S. multipunctatus*, known as the Cuckoo Catfish, sneaks its eggs into the broods of mouthbrooding cichlids, which pick them up and rear them as their own. The Walking Catfish, *Clarias batrachus,* is undismayed when its Malaysian home waters dry up; 'breathing' air with a primitive 'lung', it sets off across dry land, moving fast on its pectoral fin spines.

Catfishes can 'talk', too: lift the South American Talking Catfish, *Amblydoras hancockii,* out of the water and it will grunt at you.

In the brood care stakes, catfishes run the gamut of egg-scatterers, mouthbrooders and cave-spawners; in all cases,

Transparently beautiful – the African Glass Catfish (Kryptopterus bicirrhis).

the male guards the young. There are bubblenest-builders, too, such as *Callichthys callichthys*. In some Asian catfishes, brood care is shared. In these 'nuclear families', the male guards the eggs and both parents then look after the newly-hatched youngsters until they can fend for themselves. In *Corydoras* catfishes, the most popular of all aquarium catfish, the female picks up fertilized eggs in a cup formed by her ventral fins and then sticks them to a flat surface, usually a plant or the tank glass.

The splendid barbels of Synodontis filamentosus.

ALBINO BRONZE CORY

Corydoras aeneus
Mature size: 7cm (2.75in)
Characteristics: Albino corys
were originally spontaneous
mutations lacking black
pigment, but are
now bred to
order.

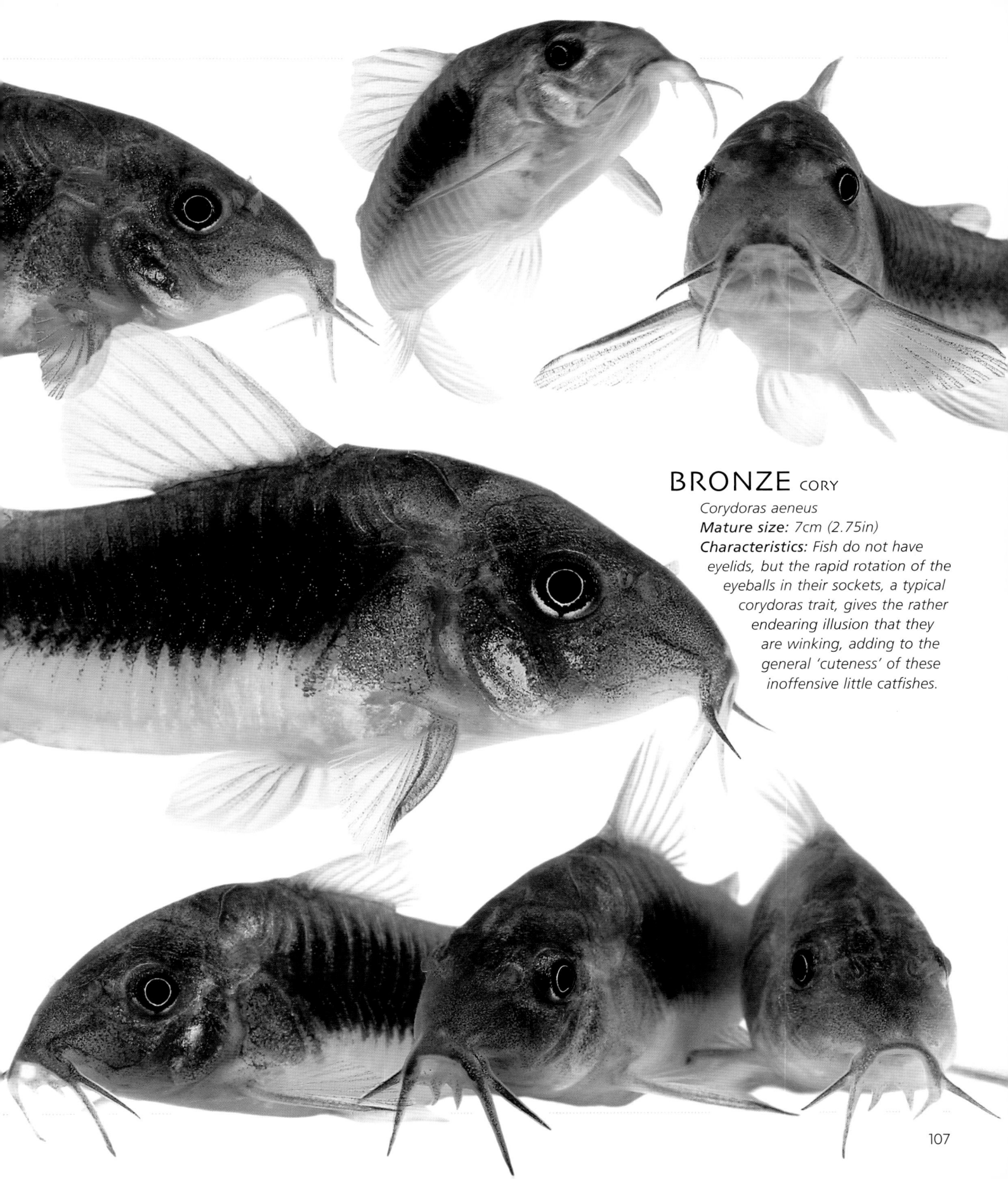

BRONZE CORY

Corydoras aeneus
Mature size: *7cm (2.75in)*
Characteristics: *Fish do not have
eyelids, but the rapid rotation of the
eyeballs in their sockets, a typical
corydoras trait, gives the rather
endearing illusion that they
are winking, adding to the
general 'cuteness' of these
inoffensive little catfishes.*

PERUVIAN
GREEN STRIPE CORY

Corydoras cf. *aeneus*
Mature size: *7cm (2.75in)*
Characteristics: *This 'strain' of the Bronze Corydoras is one of the gems among what is normally considered a rather drab fish. The enamelled scales on the flanks reflect the light and the long, undamaged barbels are a sign of fish in vigorous good health.*

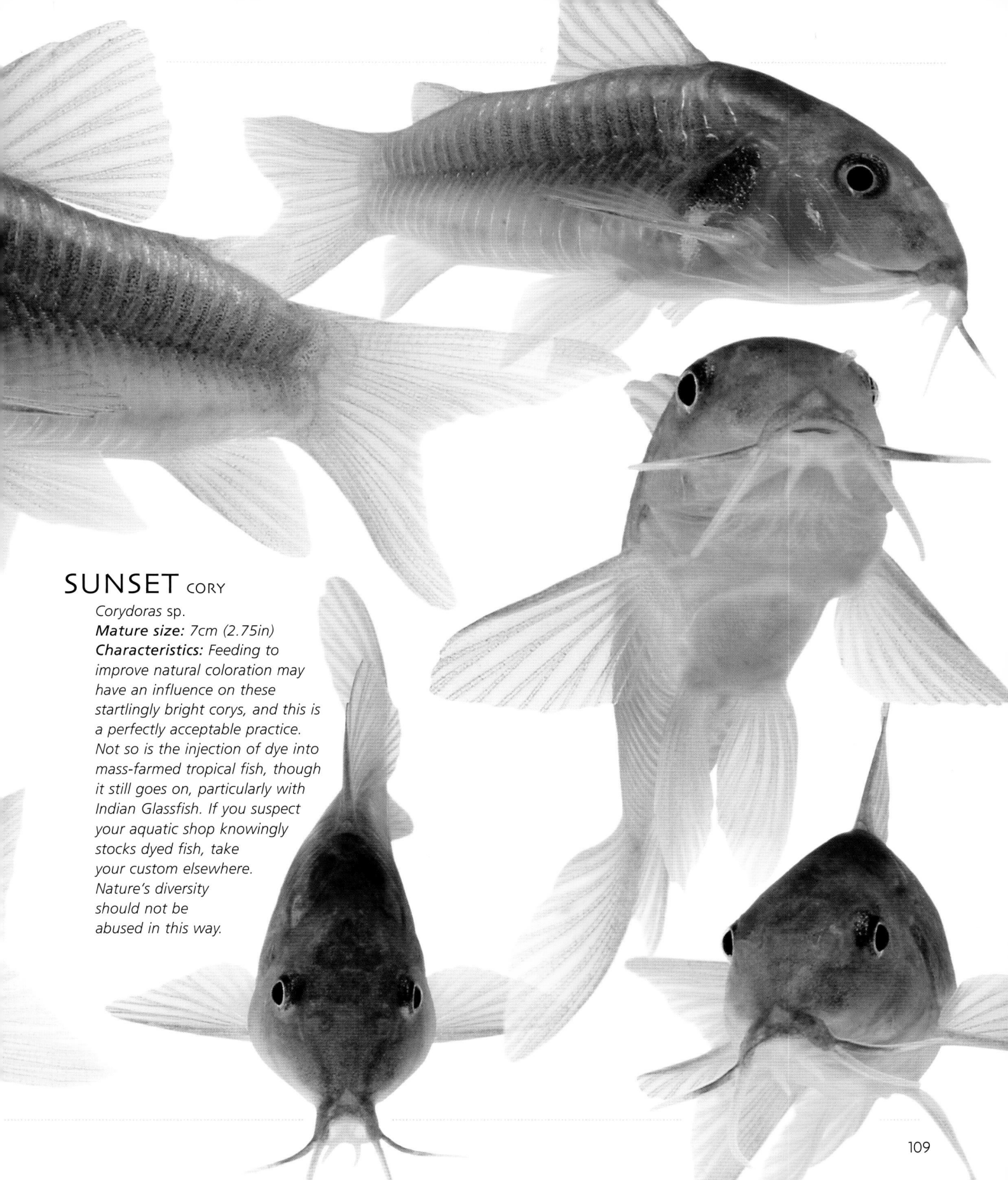

SUNSET CORY

Corydoras sp.
Mature size: *7cm (2.75in)*
Characteristics: *Feeding to improve natural coloration may have an influence on these startlingly bright corys, and this is a perfectly acceptable practice. Not so is the injection of dye into mass-farmed tropical fish, though it still goes on, particularly with Indian Glassfish. If you suspect your aquatic shop knowingly stocks dyed fish, take your custom elsewhere. Nature's diversity should not be abused in this way.*

PANDA CATFISH

Corydoras panda
Mature size: *5cm (2in)*
Characteristics: *It is easy to see how this appealing little Peruvian catfish got its name – the black mask, running from the top of the head down through the eyes, lends it a very panda-like appearance, especially when viewed head-on. To maintain their barbels in good condition, all corydoras should be kept in an aquarium with a sandy, rather than a gravel, substrate otherwise these nerve-rich sensory organs will be worn down.*

♂   ♀

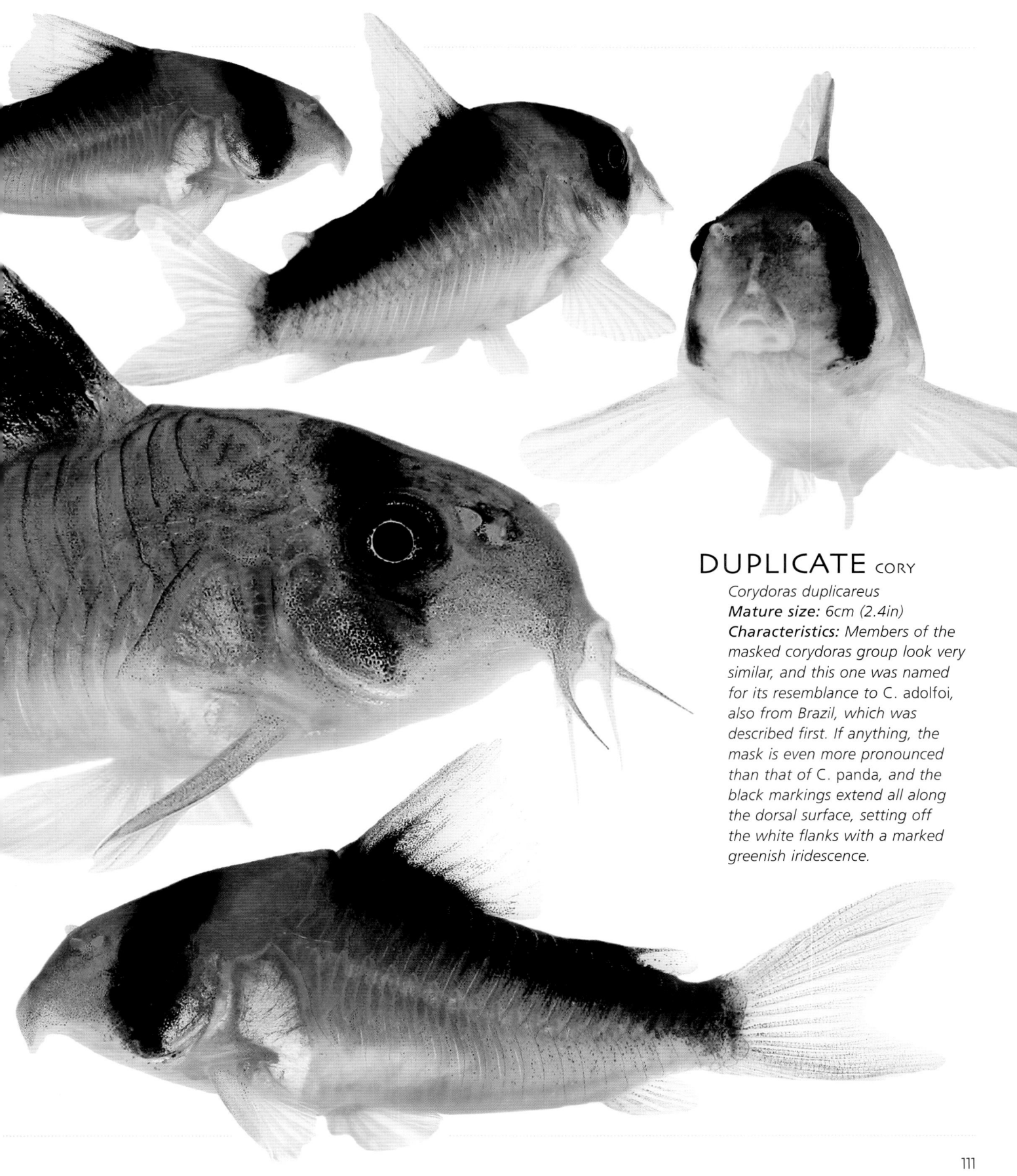

DUPLICATE CORY

Corydoras duplicareus
Mature size: *6cm (2.4in)*
Characteristics: *Members of the masked corydoras group look very similar, and this one was named for its resemblance to C. adolfoi, also from Brazil, which was described first. If anything, the mask is even more pronounced than that of C. panda, and the black markings extend all along the dorsal surface, setting off the white flanks with a marked greenish iridescence.*

STERBA'S CORY

Corydoras sterbai
Mature size: *6cm (2.4in)*
Characteristics: *Vertical bars on the caudal fin, contrasting horizontal lines of black spots on the flanks and a neatly spotted head – look closely and be amazed at the complexity of the pattern of this Brazilian cory. As in all corydoras, ripe females become quite rotund compared to males.*

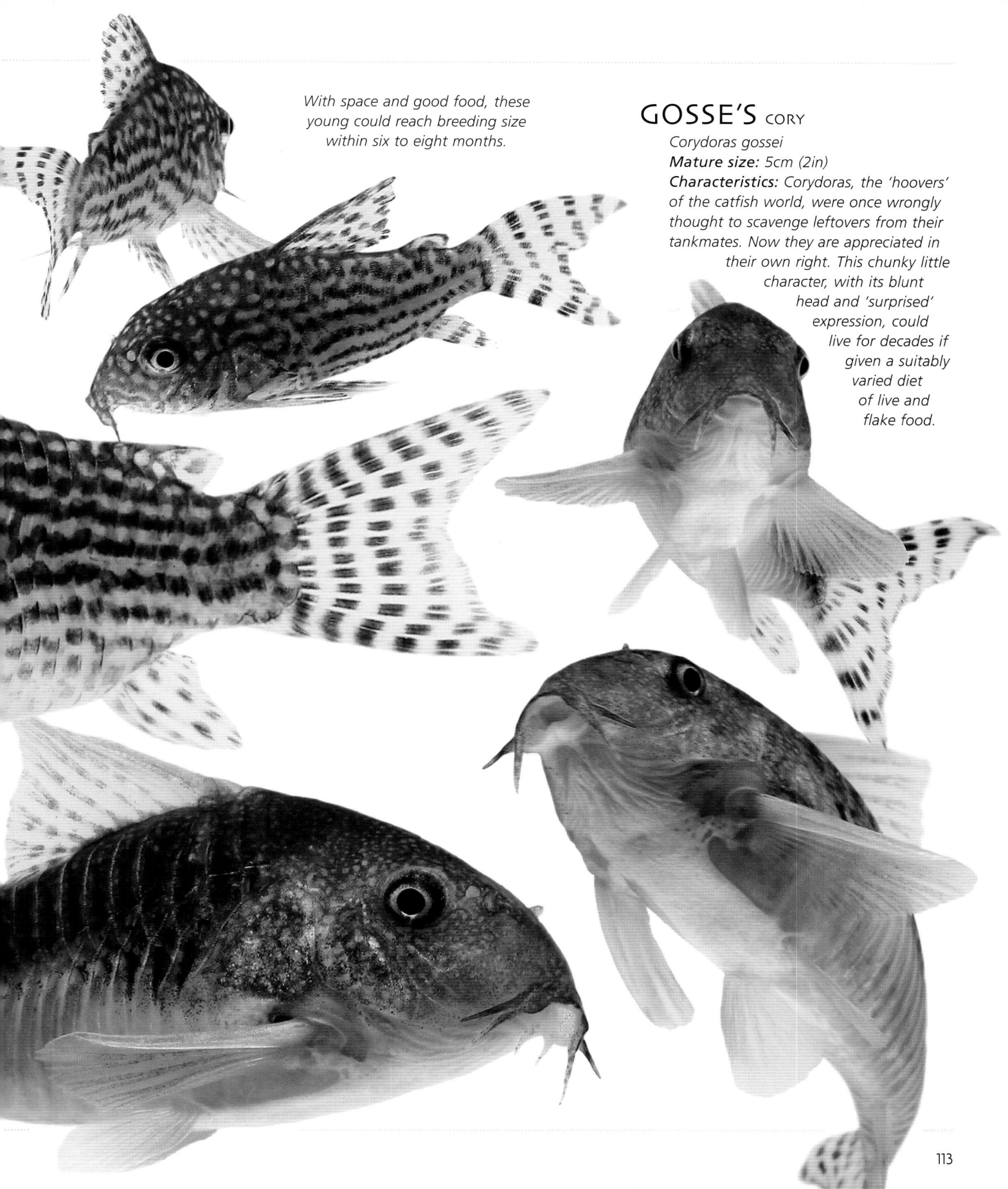

With space and good food, these young could reach breeding size within six to eight months.

GOSSE'S CORY

Corydoras gossei

Mature size: *5cm (2in)*

Characteristics: *Corydoras, the 'hoovers' of the catfish world, were once wrongly thought to scavenge leftovers from their tankmates. Now they are appreciated in their own right. This chunky little character, with its blunt head and 'surprised' expression, could live for decades if given a suitably varied diet of live and flake food.*

EMERALD CATFISH

Brochis splendens
Mature size: 7cm (2.75in)
Characteristics: The longer
dorsal fin is an instant
giveaway, showing
that these
callichthyids are not
true Corydoras, although they
are very closely related.
Brochis *are more robustly
built, deeper in the body,
with a more massive
head and a longer
snout, but in
temperament
there are no real differences
between the genera. They lay
large, adhesive eggs on flat
vertical or horizontal surfaces.*

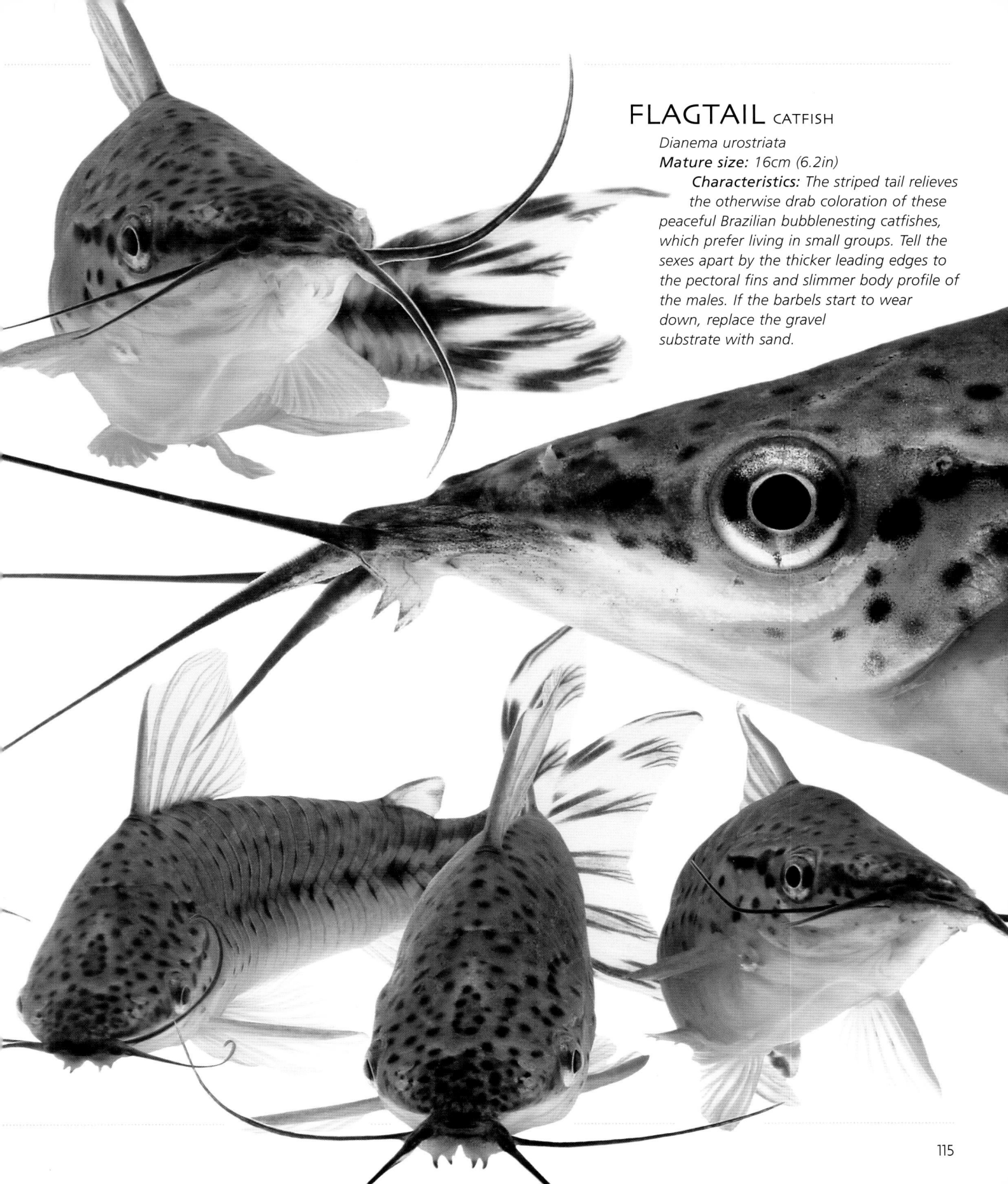

FLAGTAIL CATFISH

Dianema urostriata
Mature size: *16cm (6.2in)*
Characteristics: *The striped tail relieves the otherwise drab coloration of these peaceful Brazilian bubblenesting catfishes, which prefer living in small groups. Tell the sexes apart by the thicker leading edges to the pectoral fins and slimmer body profile of the males. If the barbels start to wear down, replace the gravel substrate with sand.*

CLOWN
SYNODONTIS

Synodontis decorus
Mature size: 24cm
(9.5in)
Characteristics:
*This droll catfish
from the Zaire River in Africa is an
aquarium natural. It has a long,
mournful face adorned with
branched barbels, dorsal fin
filament, and a pattern so sharp it
could have been painted on. But
do not mix it with Rift Lake
cichlids – water chemistry
in the two habitats
is very different.*

CUCKOO CATFISH

Synodontis multipunctatus
Mature size: *12cm (4.7in)*
Characteristics: *Why cuckoo? This multispotted synodontis from Lake Tanganyika sneaks its eggs in among those of mouth-brooding cichlids, which act as unwitting foster parents. Beautiful, as well as resourceful – look at those amazing tail markings.*

ANGEL CATFISH

Synodontis angelicus
Mature size: *5cm (2in)*
Characteristics: *When this delightful fish was first imported from Africa, it was given its common name (and a high price tag) because its markings were almost supernaturally perfect. It likes to hide under bogwood during the day, so you may not appreciate its beauty unless you feed just after lights-out and wait for it to emerge.*

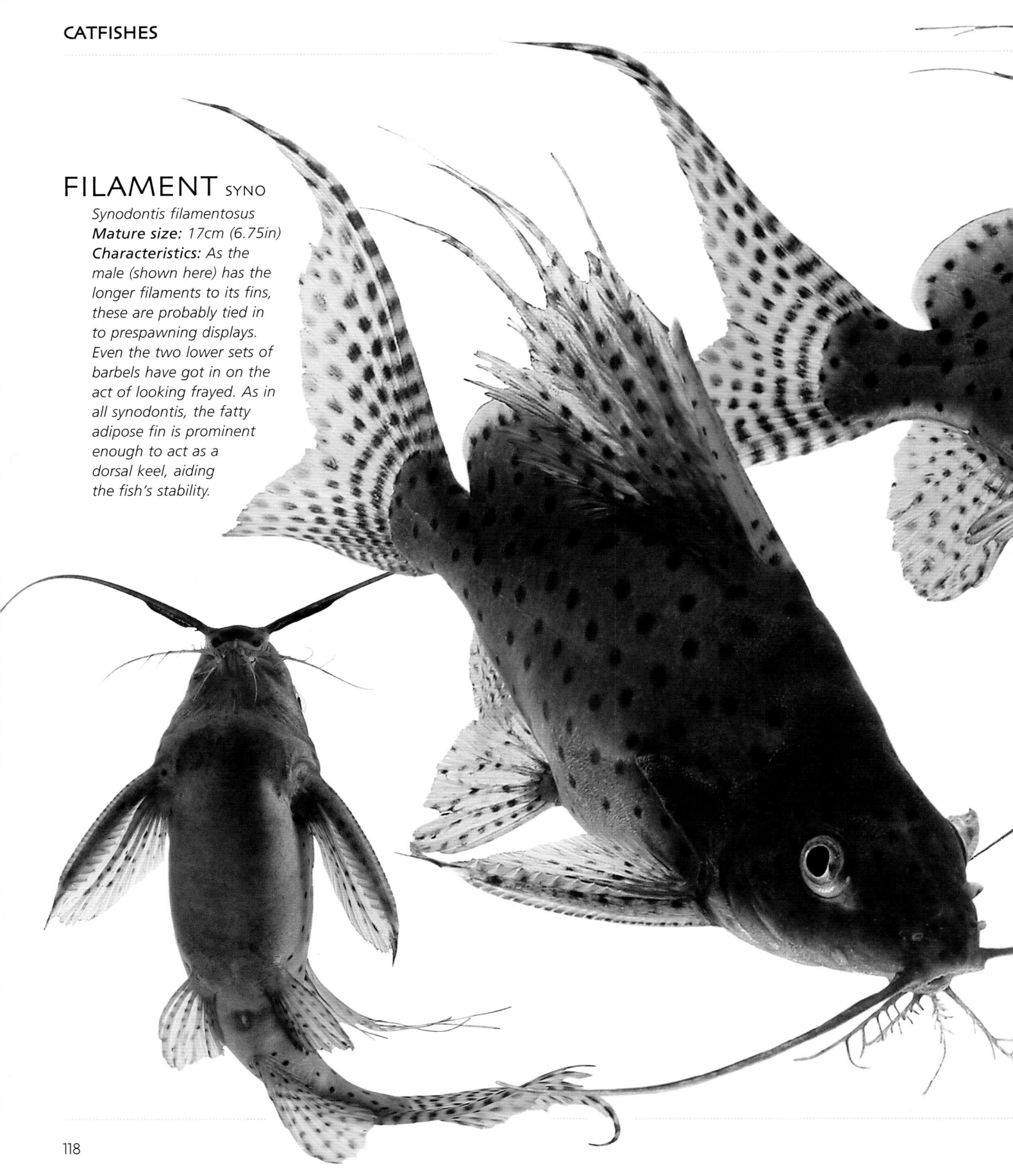

FILAMENT SYNO

Synodontis filamentosus
Mature size: *17cm (6.75in)*
Characteristics: *As the male (shown here) has the longer filaments to its fins, these are probably tied in to prespawning displays. Even the two lower sets of barbels have got in on the act of looking frayed. As in all synodontis, the fatty adipose fin is prominent enough to act as a dorsal keel, aiding the fish's stability.*

GREATER UPSIDE-DOWN
SYNODONTIS

Brachysynodontis batensoda
Mature size: *20cm (8in)*
Characteristics: *This is the less common Upside-down Catfish, and has not quite made up its mind which way up it should approach life – sometimes it swims normally, at other times it inverts. Rather squat at rest, it shows surprisingly sinuous grace as it comes up in search of food.*

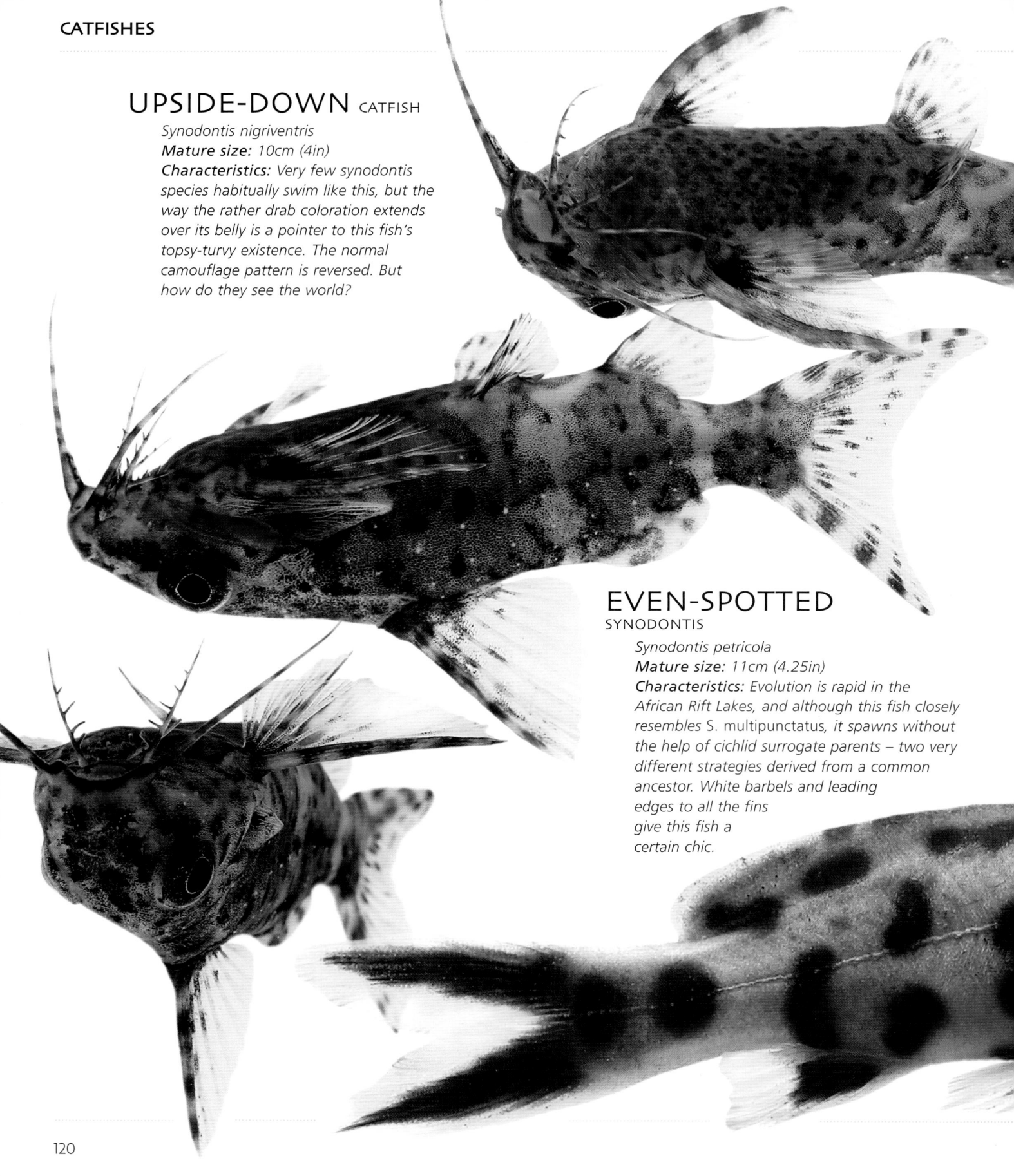

UPSIDE-DOWN CATFISH

Synodontis nigriventris
Mature size: *10cm (4in)*
Characteristics: *Very few synodontis species habitually swim like this, but the way the rather drab coloration extends over its belly is a pointer to this fish's topsy-turvy existence. The normal camouflage pattern is reversed. But how do they see the world?*

EVEN-SPOTTED SYNODONTIS

Synodontis petricola
Mature size: *11cm (4.25in)*
Characteristics: *Evolution is rapid in the African Rift Lakes, and although this fish closely resembles S. multipunctatus, it spawns without the help of cichlid surrogate parents – two very different strategies derived from a common ancestor. White barbels and leading edges to all the fins give this fish a certain chic.*

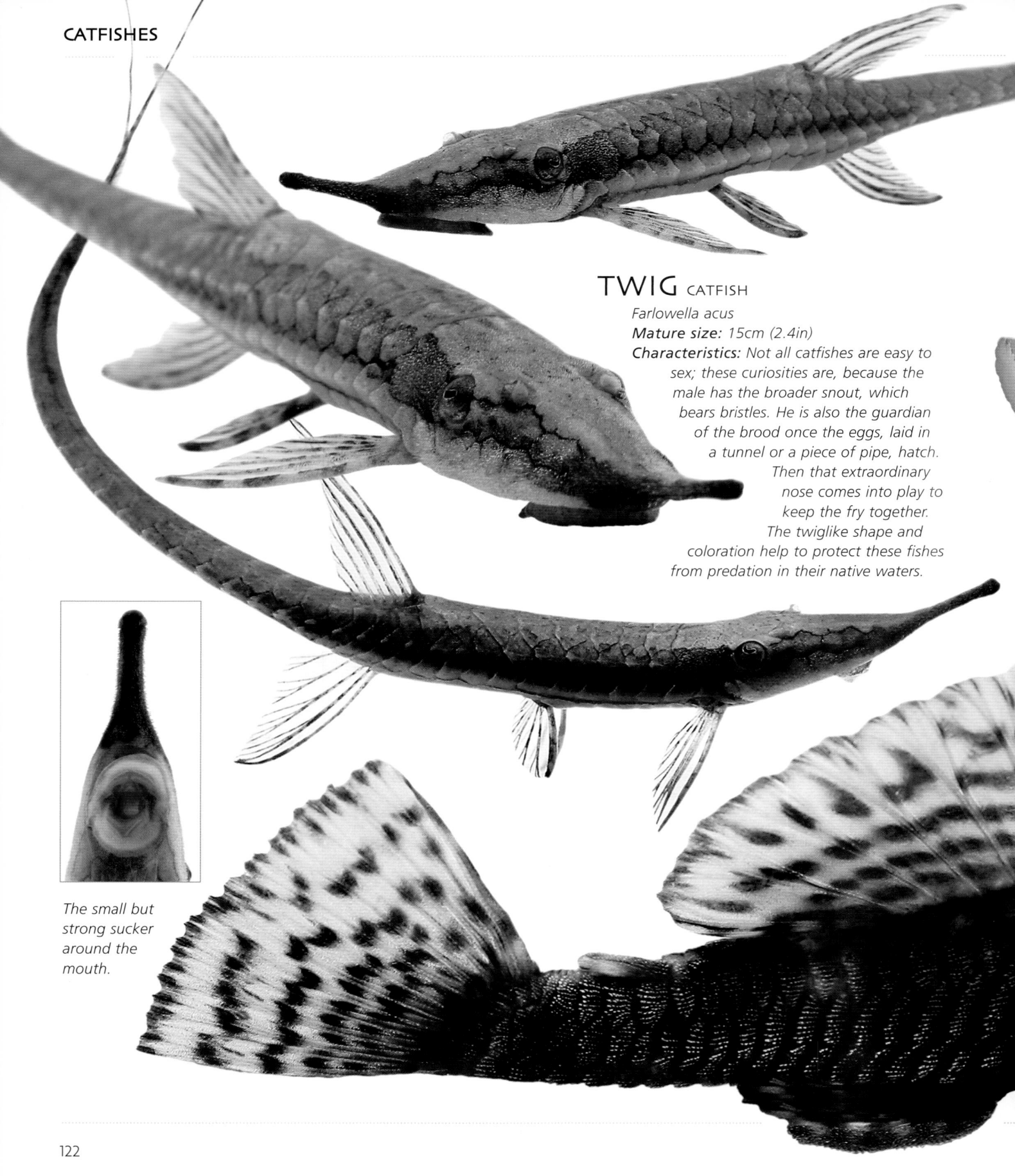

TWIG CATFISH

Farlowella acus
Mature size: *15cm (2.4in)*
Characteristics: *Not all catfishes are easy to sex; these curiosities are, because the male has the broader snout, which bears bristles. He is also the guardian of the brood once the eggs, laid in a tunnel or a piece of pipe, hatch. Then that extraordinary nose comes into play to keep the fry together. The twiglike shape and coloration help to protect these fishes from predation in their native waters.*

The small but strong sucker around the mouth.

These views show the sucker mouth on the leucistic (left) and normal forms.

BRISTLENOSE
CATFISH

Ancistrus temminckii
Mature size: *12cm (4.7in)*
Characteristics: *To a female Ancistrus, those fleshy nose bristles signal 'macho mate' – and this fearsome-looking mini combat tank proves a great dad, too, brooding a clutch of orange eggs under a rock or in a cave. These are the easiest suckermouths to spawn in an aquarium. The top fish is a leucistic (semi-albino) form.*

SPINY SUCKERMOUTH CATFISH

Isorineloricaria spinosissima
Mature size: 60cm (24in)
Characteristics: Handle this creature with care, because the rear edge of its gill covers are formed into long, thorny spikes. When moving these catfish around, it is best to pick them up wearing thick gloves, as they will entangle themselves in the usual net and damage themselves. The graceful tail and sail-like dorsal fin vie for attention with a polkadot pattern, but this may fade as the fish approaches full size.

PIMELODUS CATFISH

Pimelodus pictus
Mature size: 12cm (4.7in)
Characteristics: The spotted silvery body of the Pimelodus catfish shines like burnished metal as it swims actively around, whiskers waving. This native of Colombia, in South America, can be safely kept with similar-sized tankmates, but will treat anything Neon-sized as a welcome snack.

ZEBRA CATFISH ✳

Hypancistrus zebra
Mature size: *15cm (6in)*
Characteristics: *Luckily, the world's most popular specimen aquarium catfish is now bred commercially in the USA. Seen against a plain background the pattern is startling, but in the wild, on a pale substrate in dappled shade, these fishes can be as inconspicuous as their zebra namesakes. Males (shown here) have a spinier leading edge to the pectoral fins.*

GOLD'S PLEC

Scobinancistrus aureatus
Mature size: *30cm (12in)*
Characteristics: *So many
similar-looking South American
suckermouths are being
imported these days that
making a positive
identification can be
very difficult. To
assist, many of them
carry 'L', or location,
numbers that
pinpoint where they
are collected, and
this one is L14, from
Brazil's Rio Xingu. It is
hard not to smile as you
look at this fish, which
seems to be bathed in golden
sunlight. This example, with
the dappled body pattern
extending well into the fins,
shows just how protrusible
the suckermouth is. The
single pair of barbels on
the outer corners of the
lips are quite elongated,
as you would expect of
an animal from a fast-
flowing river, where
sensory information is
carried down rapidly on
the current and needs to
be acted upon quickly if
the fish is to obtain a meal.*

REDTAIL CATFISH

Phractocephalus hemioliopterus
Mature size: *180cm (72in)*
Characteristics: *One to admire in public aquariums, rather than try to keep at home – a cute baby is one thing, a six-foot predator quite another. But there is no denying the 'wow factor' of this creature, with its go-faster flank stripe, reddish orange propulsion unit and three wonderfully mobile pairs of barbels.*

SCARLET CATFISH

Pseudacanthicus leopardus
Mature size: *30cm (12in)*
Characteristics: *Once, all unidentified suckermouth catfishes were labelled 'plecs', but accurate identification is the key to adult size. The thorny and impregnable body protection of this fish explains its alternative common name of 'Cactus Cat'.*

YELLOW SPOT CATFISH

Parancistrus sp. L282
Mature size: *20cm (8in)*
Characteristics: *A recent import from Brazil, identified only by its L number. What a beauty it is, from all angles!*

CRYSTAL-EYE CATFISH

Hemibagrus wyckii
Mature size: *80cm (32in)*
Characteristics: *A Southeast Asian villain, jet-black, predatory and built for speed. Keep it as a pet in a tank on its own, but mind your fingers at feeding time!*

ROYAL PLEC

Panaque nigrolineatus
Mature size: *25cm (10in)*
Characteristics: *Startling zebralike facial stripes and curious omega-shaped pupils make this a show-stopping aquarium star. Rasping away at pieces of bogwood aquarium decor aids its digestion, but do not expect it to clear the tank of algae. It will much prefer sinking catfish pellets or a piece of cucumber.*

RAINBO

Adapting tropical fishes to the local mains water can be difficult: although many farmed community species (including South American tetras) will live quite happily in moderately hard, alkaline water, they need soft, acid water if they are to breed successfully.

This is not the case with Rainbowfishes, the chemistry of whose native Australasian waters closely matches what comes out of the tap in areas where the supply is drawn from chalk or limestone rocks. That, teamed with their beauty and peaceful nature, means Rainbowfishes are enjoying a surge in popularity.

There are eight families in the order Atheriformes, two of which are exclusively marine fishes; from an aquarium point of view only three others are of interest. Most species we see for sale belong to the family Melanotaenidae, from northern and eastern Australia and New Guinea. The two exceptions

Slim, subtle and streamlined sum up the elegant Threadfin Rainbowfish.

The Red Rainbowfish is deep-bodied, with simple, vivid coloration.

are the Madagascar Rainbowfish (*Bedotia geayi*) and the Celebes Rainbow (*Marosatherina ladigesi*) from Sulawesi.

A double dorsal fin is a characteristic of Rainbowfishes.

The longer, hindmost fin closely matches the anal fin in shape and coloration, giving the fish a pleasing symmetry. This is carried to extremes in the Threadfin Rainbow (*Iriatherina werneri*), males of which have long fin extensions used to display to potential mates.

Very few wild-caught Rainbowfishes are offered for sale and, unfortunately, the stunning coloration becomes muted after a few generations of captive breeding. This, and the existence of local subspecies, can make positive identification difficult. Nonetheless, the male Red Rainbow *(Glossolepis incisus)* remains a particularly striking fish, carrying the deep crimson body shade into all its finnage. It makes a superb occupant of display aquariums, where it occupies the middle layers of the water.

Rainbowfishes look best in large, well-planted tanks with a dark sandy substrate and some spotlighting supplementing the overhead tubes. Their coloration

Male Celebes Rainbowfishes with yellow fins and noses.

appears to change and shimmer as they swim from shaded into brighter areas, hence their common name.

Although *Melanotaenia* females tend to be less vivid, keeping both sexes together encourages the males to show of their best. Like the tetras, they are happiest living in shoals in the aquarium. They

will eat all types of commercially prepared foods, although their diet in the wild is made up of insects, small aquatic invertebrates and sometimes some algae.

Rainbowfish spawnings tend to be protracted, a few eggs being laid each day over a long period in plant thickets or artificial spawning mops. The fry need very fine first food, such as newly hatched brineshrimp *(Artemia).*

A young pair of popular Boesman's Rainbows; the male is the lower fish.

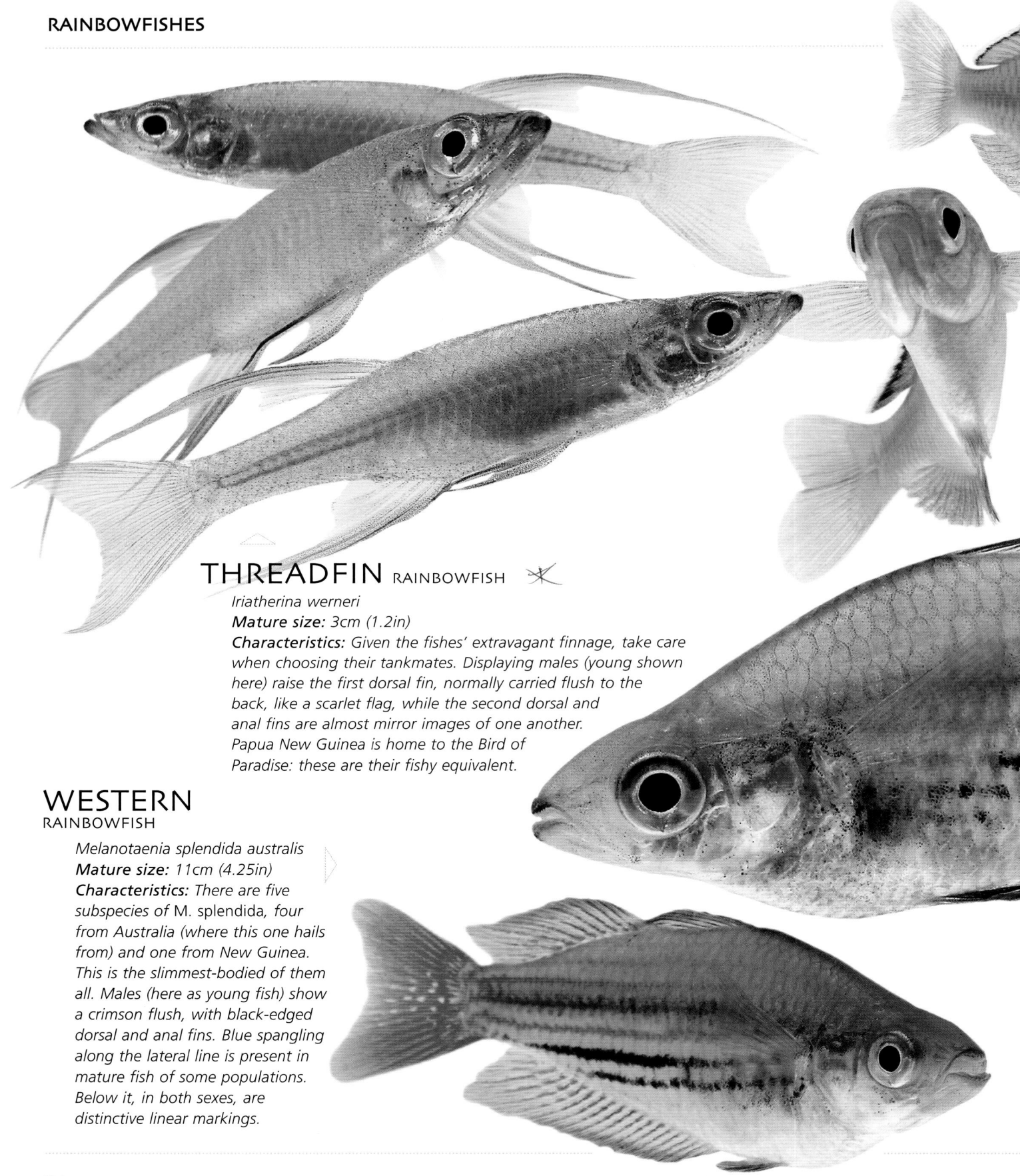

THREADFIN RAINBOWFISH

Iriatherina werneri
Mature size: *3cm (1.2in)*
Characteristics: *Given the fishes' extravagant finnage, take care when choosing their tankmates. Displaying males (young shown here) raise the first dorsal fin, normally carried flush to the back, like a scarlet flag, while the second dorsal and anal fins are almost mirror images of one another. Papua New Guinea is home to the Bird of Paradise: these are their fishy equivalent.*

WESTERN
RAINBOWFISH

Melanotaenia splendida australis
Mature size: *11cm (4.25in)*
Characteristics: *There are five subspecies of M. splendida, four from Australia (where this one hails from) and one from New Guinea. This is the slimmest-bodied of them all. Males (here as young fish) show a crimson flush, with black-edged dorsal and anal fins. Blue spangling along the lateral line is present in mature fish of some populations. Below it, in both sexes, are distinctive linear markings.*

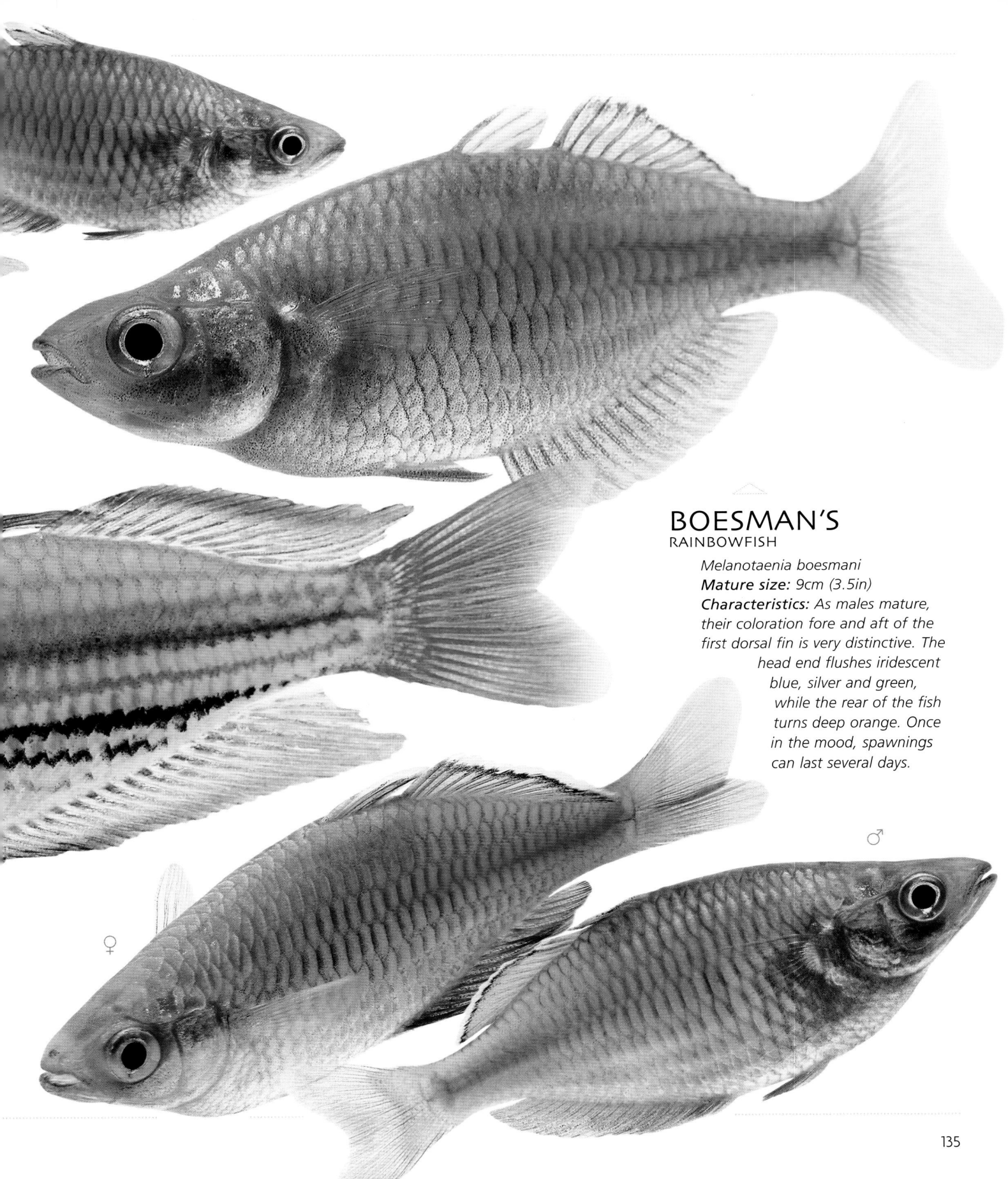

BOESMAN'S
RAINBOWFISH

Melanotaenia boesmani
Mature size: *9cm (3.5in)*
Characteristics: *As males mature, their coloration fore and aft of the first dorsal fin is very distinctive. The head end flushes iridescent blue, silver and green, while the rear of the fish turns deep orange. Once in the mood, spawnings can last several days.*

♂

♀

CELEBES
RAINBOWFISH

Marosatherina ladigesi
Mature size: *7cm (2.75in)*
Characteristics: *The Celebes
Rainbowfish, from Sulawesi,
belongs to a family with several
representatives from brackish
waters. The blue flank reminds
us of the Neon Tetra, and
the finnage of mature
males is striking –
rays of the second
dorsal and anal fin
are elongated and
separated. Females are
drabber, but without their
presence in the tank you
will not see males
display to their best
advantage. These
are young fish.*

♀

♂

RED
RAINBOWFISH

Glossolepis incisus
Mature size: *12cm (4.7in)*
Characteristics: *Rainbowfishes have a lot going for them – they are peaceable, adaptable, not fussy about their food and fairly easy to breed if you give them a spawning mop or a thickly planted tank. In this New Guinean species, the males (shown here) become quite deep-bodied as they mature and their coloration intensifies when the ladies are around.*

LOACHES

Clown prince –
Botia macracantha
with its motley markings.

streamlining helps the fish hug the riverbed. If you are looking for a peaceful loach, *Botia macracantha* is hard to beat. Droll, dramatically banded and gregarious, it is usually imported small, but can eventually attain 30cm (12in). Aquarium spawnings are extremely rare; it is thought that breeding is triggered by the arrival of the rains.

Some botias are quite sturdy and high-backed (*Botia morleti*, Hora's Loach), while others are slim and elongated. Taking matters to extremes, though, are the worm-like Kuhli loaches (*Pangio* spp.) which, for some reason, are always recommended as community fishes. But they are so secretive that once in the tank you rarely catch more than fleeting

glimpses of them – and since they are more agile than a greased eel, it is virtually impossible ever to net them out again.

It's black, it's red-tailed, but the Red-tailed Black Shark is a shark in name only.

'Loach' is a catch-all name for two families of aquarium fishes – Balitoridae (river and hillstream loaches) and the far more popular Cobitidae (including the familiar Clown loach, belonging to the genus *Botia*). Members of the latter tend to have a flat belly profile and an 'aquadynamic' snout adorned with prominent barbels, which are used to root out invertebrate food items. When facing into a current, this

The Hillstream Loach (Gastromyzon sp.) is ideally shaped for its fast-flowing habitat.

& SHARKS

Many similar-looking banded loaches are regularly imported with only sketchy identification. Some of these can be very territorial, and it is definitely a case of keeping one per tank – then only if there is plenty of cover for them in the form of rocks and bogwood. To avoid conflict in the aquarium, steer clear of any loach that is marked like a tiger or a zebra.

'Sharks' are not really sharks at all, but Asian members of the carp family that bear a superficial resemblance to the marine predators in general body shape and, in particular, the triangular dorsal fin. This illusion is most pronounced in the Red-tailed Black Shark *(Epalzeorhynchos bicolor)*, because the velvet-black of the body extends into the dorsal fin. This, and the clearly delineated red caudal fin, gives it a guaranteed place in the community aquarium although, like other members of its genus, it can be grumpy and may pick on smaller individuals.

Tiger barbs are common targets, possibly because they are mistaken for other sharks. Little physical damage is inflicted, but once a Red-tail gets a complex about any of its tankmates it is a case of more or less constant harassment.

No such bullying stains the character of the two Flying Foxes. *Crossocheilus siamensis* (Siamese Flying Fox) is more concerned with eating algae than scrapping, and the lookalike *Epalzeorhynchos kalopterus* (Flying Fox) makes only small inroads into the greenery and is an inoffensive enough fish.

Normally placid, these Flying Foxes are living up to their name.

RED-FINNED SHARK

Epalzeorhynchos frenatus
Mature size: *15cm (6in)*
Characteristics: *This slimline shark, also known as the Ruby Shark, is an active midwater swimmer, and more peaceable than the RTBS. All the fins are orange-red (brighter in males) with a darker diamond-shaped blotch on the wrist of the tail. Dark barbels stand out beside a characteristic facial stripe. They are spawned commercially in ponds in Thailand, but aquarium breeding success is rare.*

RED-TAILED BLACK SHARK

Epalzeorhynchos bicolor
Mature size: *12cm (4.7in)*
Characteristics: *Not really a shark, of course, but a member of the carp family, although the triangular dorsal fin does give it the look of 'Jaws'. One only per tank, as it does not much like the company of its own species. It originates from Thailand, and farmed specimens rarely attain the size of wild fish. The sensory barbels are used to locate small food items, scraped off rocks with hard, bony mouthparts. The RTBS, as it is commonly known, appreciates a territory of its own, such as a rock cave or plant thicket.*

ALBINO SHARK

Epalzeorhynchos frenatus
Mature size: *15cm (6in)*
Characteristics: *Albino forms of some aquarium fish are very popular. In true albinism there is a complete lack of the black pigment, melanin, and the eyes are red. In these examples you can still detect faint traces of the caudal spot. True albinos seldom reach maturity in the wild because they are too conspicuous.*

✳SILVER SHARK

Balantiocheilus melanopterus
Mature size: *35cm (14in)*
Characteristics: *These sporty-looking silver fish with lemon yellow-and-black finnage are extremely active members of the carp family, and look best in a shoal. They are great jumpers, so cover their tank closely. Aquarium spawnings are rare, but Silver Sharks are bred commercially in the Far East by pituitary injection, which takes pressure off the wild population. They are peaceable fishes that prefer some vegetable matter in their diet.*

CLOWN LOACH

Botia macracantha

Mature size: *30cm (12in)*

Characteristics: *Nobody knows quite why Clown Loaches have the odd habit of lying on their sides for hours on end, but it seems to be quite normal. Fish bought in aquatic shops are usually babies or juveniles, and few people realize how large they can grow, given enough space. Their droll, banded pattern, streamlined yet sturdy bodies and relatively peaceful nature make them popular aquarium subjects. However, they can be very sensitive to tank medications.*

FLYING FOX

Epalzeorhynchos kalopterus
Mature size: *15cm (6in)*
Characteristics: *From its streamlined shape, you would expect this Asian cyprinid to be a shoaling swimmer, but in fact it is a solitary character that spends most of its time at rest amid plants. It will eat algae, and is often bought for that purpose, but many other fishes perform the task better, including the Siamese Flying Fox featured at bottom right. On the plus side, it is peaceable and rather attractive in a quiet sort of way.*

SIAMESE FLYING FOX

Crossocheilus siamensis
Mature size: *14cm (5.5in)*
Characteristics: *This fish is often
confused with the 'other' Flying Fox,
even by importers, but if thread algae
is a problem in your aquarium it is well
worth tracking down. A failsafe ID point is the
absence of barbels. This is altogether a drabber
and more thickset fish that earns its place by
virtue of what it does, rather than
what it looks like.*

GOLD ZEBRA LOACH

Botia histrionica
Mature size: *6.5cm (2.5in)*
Characteristics: *Formerly Botia dario, the Gold Zebra (or Bengal) Loach from India is intensively tank-bred in Far Eastern fish farms, but rarely spawned in the aquarium.*

POLKADOT LOACH

Botia rostrata
Mature size: *6cm (2.4in)*
Characteristics: *This moderately belligerent fish from India and Burma is also known as the Ladder Loach. Females are larger and have fewer light blotches – not that these fishes have been successfully spawned in aquariums.*

TRIANGLE LOACH

Mesonomacheilus triangularis
Mature size: *8cm (3.2in)*
Characteristics: *Pattern varies greatly among individuals of this Northern Indian loach which, like many of its tribe, is most active after dark.*

SKUNK LOACH

Botia morleti
Mature size: *22cm (8.5in)*
Characteristics: *Few people realize the size attained by these solidly built fish as sexually mature adults. Their common name comes from the dorsal stripe, but their temperament is closer to that of the peaceable Clown Loach. They are also known as Hora's Loach.*

KUHLI LOACH

Pangio kuhlii sumatranus
Mature size: *11cm (4.25in)*
Characteristics: *You never quite know what you are getting with Kuhli Loaches – several species are offered under the common name. All bear a defensive spine just behind the eye and are secretive and next-to-impossible to catch, yet they remain an aquarium staple. Wild fish are said to lay large, green, floating eggs; females are fuller-bodied.*

✷REDLINE TORPEDOFISH

Crossocheilus denisonii
Mature size: *15cm (6in)*
Characteristics: *By far the most striking member of its genus, this Indian fish sports a crimson pennant marking that runs along the flank from eye to dorsal fin, and echoes of the other body coloration in the deeply forked tail. It is not often seen in the hobby, which is a shame, because it has no vices, eats the usual fare and will not pick fights with its tankmates.*

BLACK SHARK

Labeo chrysophekadion
Mature size: 60cm (24in)
Characteristics: Young specimens of this
most 'sharklike' of sharks are a funereal
matt black, but as they mature they develop
an underlying bronze tint. They are grumpy
rather than overtly aggressive. Usually
bought small, they quickly outstrip
other fish in a community
tank, to which they are
not really suited.
Black Sharks eat
plenty of green
matter, so feed
them algae wafers, plus
flake and freeze-dried
insect foods.

There is never a dull moment in a tank where barbs swim. Active and gregarious, a shoal of barbs provides movement and interest in the midwater zone of a community aquarium.

BARBS

In basic outline, barbs are everyone's idea of a 'typical' fish. These members of the worldwide carp family Cyprinidae all show the typical streamlined shape of midwater shoaling fishes, and their lifestyle does not require bizarre adaptations to deal with a challenging habitat.

The term 'barb' is unscientific, but we understand it to mean fish of the genus *Barbus* from both Africa and Asia (the old generic name *Puntius* is still seen in the aquarium trade). One or two other examples, such as the Tinfoil Barb *(Barbodes schwanenfeldi)* and Hard-lipped Barb *(Osteochilus hasselti)* sneak into this category, too, but these are large fish that often end up being re-homed in public aquariums when they outgrow their quarters. Most barbs do not present us with such a problem.

Barbs feed on small aquatic insects and crustaceans and some plant matter. There are no predators to worry about in this group, although some species can

A rather surprised-looking African Striped Barb (Barbus lineatus).

A 'burnished' Copper Rosy Barb (Barbus conchonius).

be boisterous when they are kept with long-finned tankmates. Tiger Barbs *(Barbus tetrazona tetrazona)* have the reputation of being fin-nippers, but in shoals of six or more this tendency is toned down.

With their bright coloration and iridescent scales, flashing in the light as a shoal twists and turns, Asian barbs are aquarium naturals. Their common names often give clues as to their markings – Spanner, Black Ruby,

Leptobarbus hoevenii – a largish barb-like fish from Southeast Asia. The inset view shows the fine barbels.

Checker and Five-banded Barbs. While Asian barbs are vibrant, African species are subtler propositions. The small, exquisite *Barbus jae* is rose-tinted with neat lateral banding, while the Butterfly Barb *(Barbus hulstaerti)* best shows off its contrasting black, silver and yellow markings against a dark tank background.

Long-finned variant barbs of the common aquarium species – such as the Copper Rosy Barb – are the result of commercial breeding, and one of them – the Schubert's, or Golden Barb – is unknown in the wild. That adds a touch of mystery to these otherwise uncomplicated fishes.

Barbs are egg-scatterers, showing no parental care – as potential prey, the adults cannot stay around to look after their broods, so they play a percentage game. Only a very few eggs, adhering to fine-leaved plants or resting in the substrate, survive to maturity.

However, it is habitat deprivation, not natural predation, that threatens some species in the wild. The Cherry Barb *(Barbus titteya)* of Sri Lanka, hangs on thanks to conservation schemes that can easily fail during periods of political unrest, yet it is bred by the million in Far Eastern fish farms.

Exuberant Tiger Barbs. Their charm offensive easily overcomes a reputation for fin-nipping.

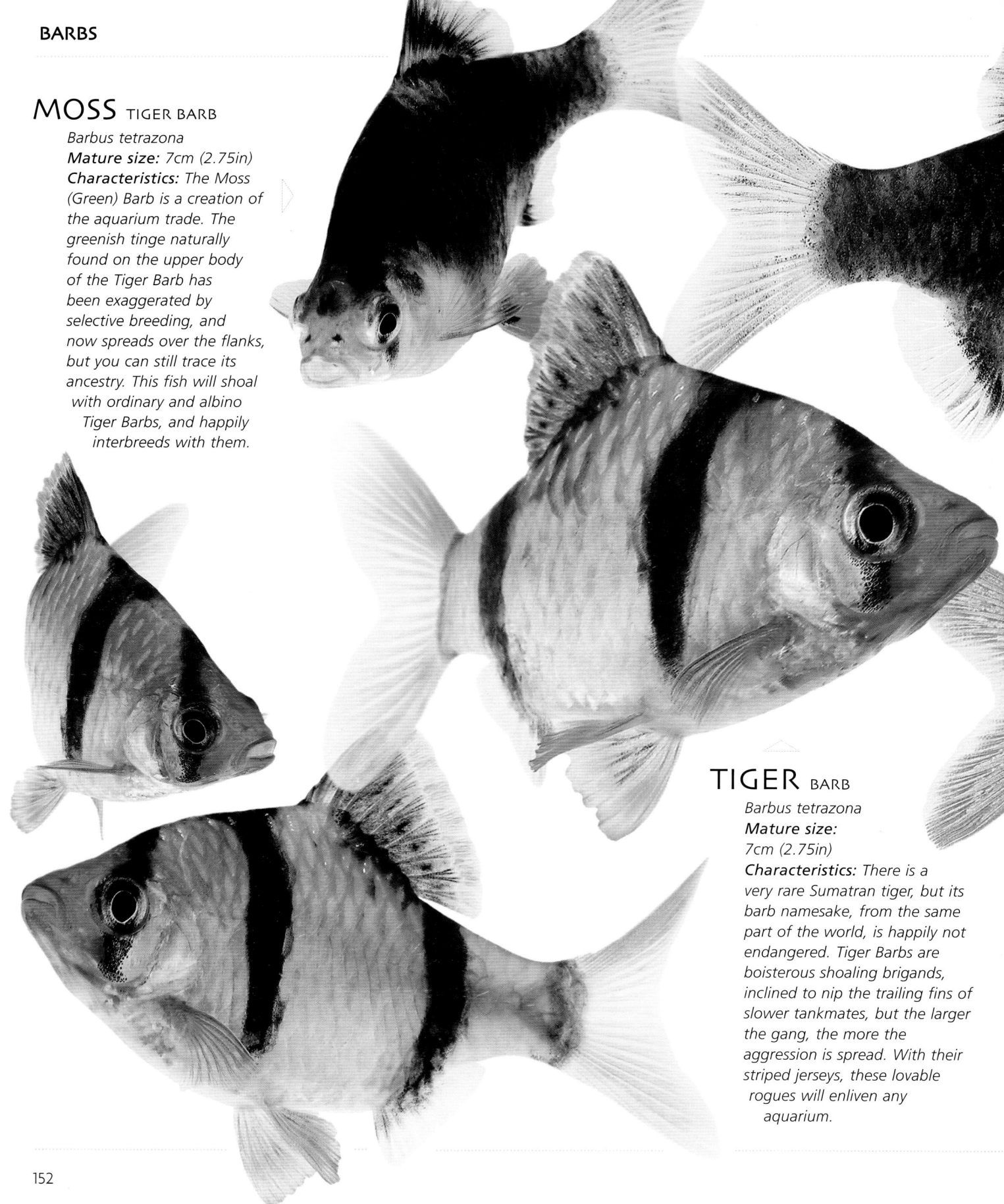

MOSS TIGER BARB

Barbus tetrazona
Mature size: *7cm (2.75in)*
Characteristics: *The Moss (Green) Barb is a creation of the aquarium trade. The greenish tinge naturally found on the upper body of the Tiger Barb has been exaggerated by selective breeding, and now spreads over the flanks, but you can still trace its ancestry. This fish will shoal with ordinary and albino Tiger Barbs, and happily interbreeds with them.*

TIGER BARB

Barbus tetrazona
Mature size: *7cm (2.75in)*
Characteristics: *There is a very rare Sumatran tiger, but its barb namesake, from the same part of the world, is happily not endangered. Tiger Barbs are boisterous shoaling brigands, inclined to nip the trailing fins of slower tankmates, but the larger the gang, the more the aggression is spread. With their striped jerseys, these lovable rogues will enliven any aquarium.*

ALBINO TIGER BARB

Barbus tetrazona
Mature size: *7cm (2.75in)*
Characteristics: *These are not true albinos, but a 'leucistic' form of the Tiger Barb in which the eyes remain black. For some reason, these fish are not as aggressive as their naturally pigmented cousins.*

COPPER
ROSY BARB

♀

♂

Barbus conchonius
Mature size: *15cm (6in)*
Characteristics: *Long a popular aquarium fish, the Rosy Barb is named for the reddish tinge that suffuses the silvery flanks, and intensifies when pairs are ready to spawn, which they do by scattering eggs among plants. This farmed variant displays elongated finnage which, in some company, can turn it from a potential fin-worrier into a victim itself. Note the gold-edged black spot forward of the tail. These undemanding fish will eat almost anything, but appreciate some live food. They shoal from midwater downwards.*

CHERRY BARB

Barbus titteya
Mature size: *5cm (2in)*
Characteristics: *The common name of these peaceable little gems from Sri Lanka comes from the deep red livery donned by the males at spawning time. Wild-caught specimens show the best coloration, but these are rare in the hobby because their habitat is under threat. Luckily, though, Cherry Barbs are extensively farmed for the hobby. They scatter eggs in plant thickets, but tend to eat them. Keep them in small shoals, with plenty of cover. Like most commercially produced barbs, they will adapt to prevailing water conditions, but soft, slightly acid water is best for breeding.*

ROSY BARB

Barbus conchonius
Mature size: *15cm (6in)*
Characteristics: *Being of the same species, long- and normal-finned Rosy Barbs will readily interbreed. If you want fishes true to type, obtain a wild-caught pair for spawning purposes. These will be more expensive, but likely to get closer to full adult size than generations of mass-produced, farmed examples. There is something comfortingly appealing about these chunky, rose-hued barbs that has endeared them to generations of fishkeepers.*

STRIPED BARB

Barbus lineatus
Mature size: *12cm (4.7in)*
Characteristics: *Males of this barb from Africa's Zaire Basin are slim and darkly pinstriped, while females are less distinctly marked, and much more rotund in their gravid state. This is quite an easy barb to spawn in plant thickets, and fry are numbered in thousands. Note the large eyes and long, whiskery barbels.*

RED-FINNED
CIGAR SHARK

Leptobarbus hoevenii
Mature size: 50cm (20in)
Characteristics: This is a rewarding Southeast Asian fish for large community tanks but, as an active midwater swimmer, it requires plenty of space to realize its full growth potential. The red, deeply forked, rounded tail lobes, streamlined shape and lips accented in black are points to appreciate in an otherwise subtle fish. The sexes are indistinguishable.

ARULIUS BARB

Barbus arulius
Mature size: 12cm (4.7in)
Characteristics: The bigger this Indian barb grows, the better it looks – males develop very elongated dorsal fin rays, and both sexes put on a show of subtle body coloration shot through with green, blue and violet, barred in black. This robust and thickset fish is easy to spawn and unfussy about what it eats, although live insect food is always welcome.

Enter the weird and wonderful world of the oddballs. You would be pushed to invent them in your wildest fantasies, but however strange they seem, nothing in Nature happens by accident.

ODDBA

What qualifies a fish as an 'oddball'? On lifestyle alone, the scope is limitless; what are we to make, for instance, of the Lake Malawi cichlid *Nimbochromis polystigma*? It lies on its side, looking just like a dead and decaying fish, only to spring to life and engulf bystanders – a case of 'prey' turned predator.

Yet that candidate somehow does not qualify. Fishkeepers tend to make snap visual judgments, and oddballs challenge our concept of what 'normal' fish should look like. Consider the Pufferfish *(Tetraodon biocellatus)*, wide-eyed and cute. Yet parts of the fish contain a deadly nerve toxin. Threaten it and it inflates with water to a size most predators cannot handle.

Many other fish carry bizarre weaponry. Freshwater Stingrays *(Potamotrygon* spp.), like their marine counterparts, have barbed, poisonous spines in their whiplike tails, and we have all heard of the

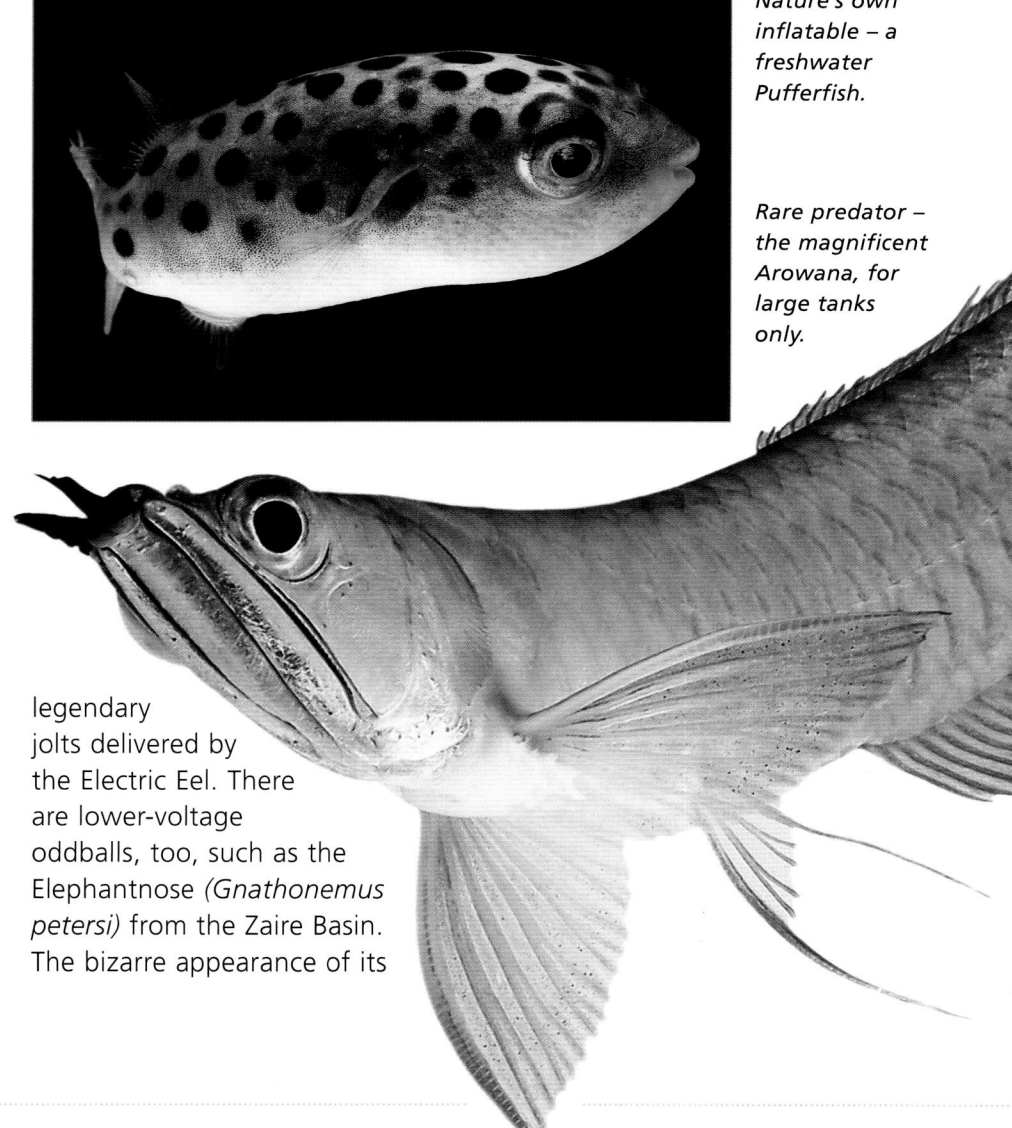

Nature's own inflatable – a freshwater Pufferfish.

Rare predator – the magnificent Arowana, for large tanks only.

legendary jolts delivered by the Electric Eel. There are lower-voltage oddballs, too, such as the Elephantnose *(Gnathonemus petersi)* from the Zaire Basin. The bizarre appearance of its

LLS

*Swamp creature –
a Spotted Garpike from
the USA, unchanged
since prehistoric times.*

trunklike snout alone is enough to stop us in our tracks, and an electric organ in the wrist of its tail has the same effect on territorial rivals. Cast an eye over the Bichirs *(Polypterus* spp.*)* and their relative, the eel-like Reedfish *(Erpetoichthys calabaricus)*. Real oddities these, as they perch on their ventral fins waiting for prey, looking like creatures from a primeval swamp.

How about the African Butterflyfish *(Pantodon buchholzi)*? Its extravagant, filamentous fins spread wide, it hangs motionless for hours under the surface. Yet when prey approaches, it can muster a blistering turn of speed. It belongs to the primitive order Osteoglossiformes (bony tongue fishes), which happens to include many other oddballs. There is the Silver Arowana *(Osteoglossum bicirrhosum)* from Amazonia, with its huge, bladelike body and forward-jutting barbels; the world's largest freshwater fish, the massive Piracuru *(Arapaima gigas)*; and the African and Asian Knifefishes, propelled along by waves from an anal fin that runs almost the full length of the body.

Many larger oddballs are carnivores, but the supremely ugly and characterful Giant Gourami *(Osphronemus gorami)*, at 71cm (28in), is a strict vegetarian. Juveniles, like those of many fishes in this section, give few clues to their eventual size or adult appearance, so beware of impulse buying.

For reasons of size, temperature, feeding and water requirements, some oddballs are best left to the specialist fishkeeper, but anyone with an eye for the bizarre will still find plenty of suitable material at their aquatic store.

Baleful beast. Snakeheads are bad news for anything smaller that swims.

BUTTERFLYFISH

Pantodon buchholzi
Mature size: 10cm (4in)
Characteristics: Surely flying fish are found only in the oceans? Then what can we make of this oddity, pectoral fins spread like the wings of an early monoplane? The paired ventral fins are equally strange, each divided into four long filaments. So still does this fish lie that it could be a mirage reflected in the surface mirror. It is a different story at night, when this predator wakes and seeks out small fish or aquatic insects. The Butterflyfish is found in forest pools in tropical West Africa. When startled, it can leap from the water and glide several yards, so obviously it needs a large tank with a close-fitting lid. It is almost impossible to wean pantodon off live food items, but as long as its tankmates are too large to be engulfed by its large upturned mouth, it is a peaceable fish to keep. Up to 400 large, floating eggs are laid, but reports of captive breeding are rare.

SILVER AROWANA

Osteoglossum bicirrhosum
Mature size: *120cm (48in)*
Characteristics: *Arowanas look prehistoric, and are indeed members of an ancient order of fishes. When the mouth of this bony tongue fish from Amazonia is closed, the head appears compact and wedge-shaped. But when the sensitive barbels (below) detect the movement of insects on the surface, the jaws open wide to engulf them. As a prized occupant of a very large aquarium, either on its own or with tankmates too*

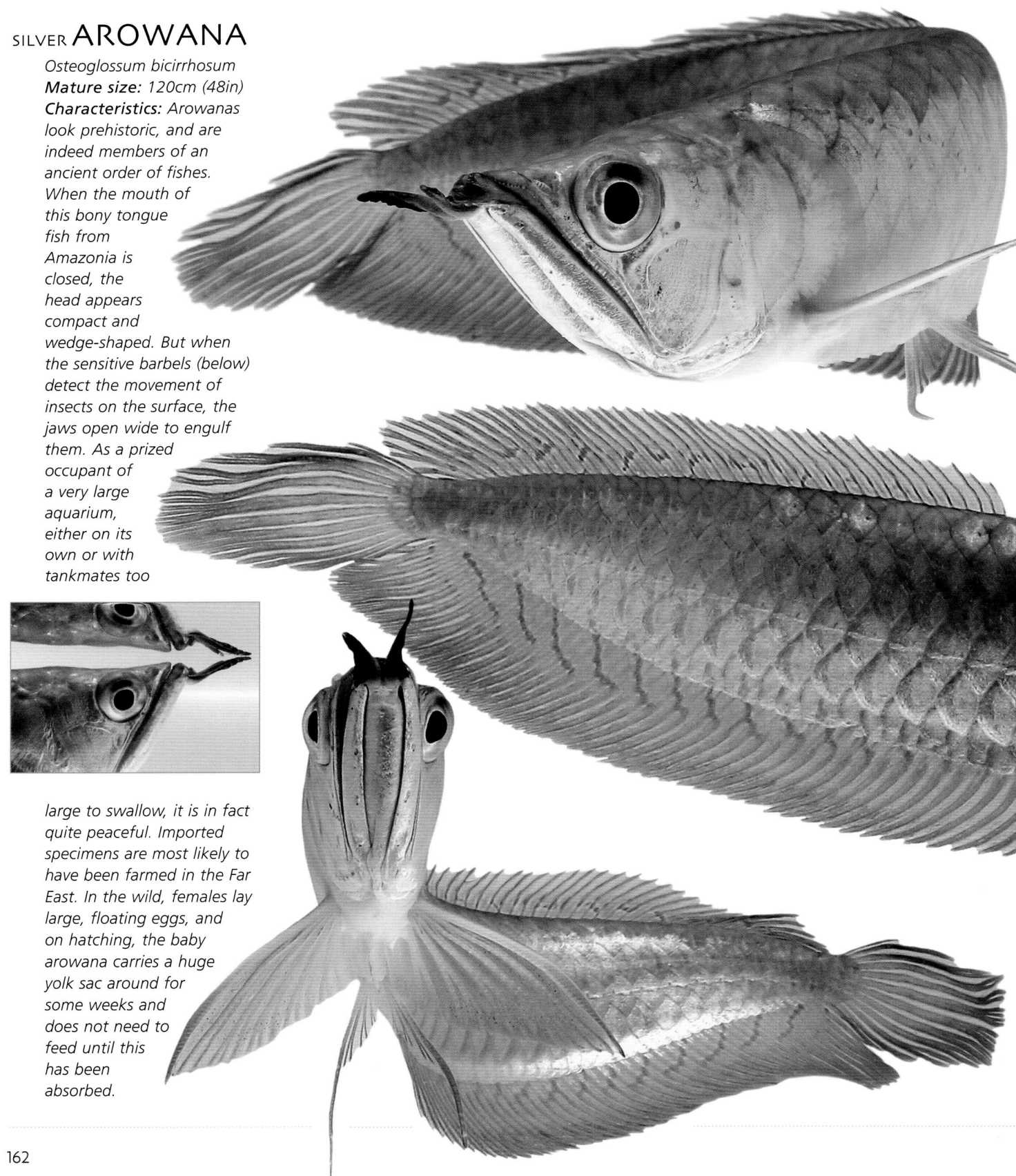

large to swallow, it is in fact quite peaceful. Imported specimens are most likely to have been farmed in the Far East. In the wild, females lay large, floating eggs, and on hatching, the baby arowana carries a huge yolk sac around for some weeks and does not need to feed until this has been absorbed.

SNAKEHEAD

Channa asiatica
Mature size: *30cm (12in)*
Characteristics: *A southern Asian 'pet' fish of some charm, and interesting for the male's habit of guarding clutches of floating eggs. All snakeheads possess a labyrinth organ for breathing atmospheric air, and are very tenacious of life. The snakehead is best kept on its own in a large specimen tank, as it is a piscivore through and through.*

RED SNAKEHEAD

Channa micropeltes
Mature size: *100cm (39in)*
Characteristics: *The Red Snakehead, often imported as a cute, striped baby only a few inches long, is the ultimate catch-out for aquarists. As it grows, its coloration and pattern become more subdued, but there is no denying that a mature specimen, which will soon come to recognize its owner, is an aquarium talking point.*

BLACK GHOST KNIFEFISH

Apteronotus albifrons
Mature size: *50cm (20in)*
Characteristics: *South American Indians fear these fishes as the spirits of drowned fishermen, and the Black Ghost Knifefish is indeed weird. Just look at the doglike face, the banded tail, which looks as though it belongs to another creature, and the massive anal fin that propels the fish backwards or forwards with a wavelike motion. A close relative is the Electric Eel, but the rather weak field generated by the Black Ghost is used only for navigation.*

CLOWN KNIFEFISH

Notopterus chitala
Mature size: *100cm (39in)*
Characteristics: *Despite its engaging ocellated markings, prey fish do not find this Southeast Asian oddity very amusing – it is a dawn and dusk hunter that superficially resembles its companion on this page, but is only distantly related. Again there is the long anal fin, but this time a small dorsal fin, too. Keep it alone, in dim light, and do not startle it – like most bullies, it is a coward at heart.*

Note how the position of the tiny mouth on the 'trunk' varies in the two species. Elephantnoses use these probes to grub around in soft substrates for food.

ELEPHANTNOSE

Gnathonemus petersi
Mature size: *23cm (9in)*
Characteristics: *These African oddities should really be called 'Elephant Mouths'. The adaptation is a nerve-rich probe used to locate small live food items in sunken leaf litter. Mormyrids, as they are also known, generate electricity in the wrist of the tail, the field marking out their territories.*

MARBLED ELEPHANTNOSE

Campylomormyrus tamandua
Mature size: *43cm (17in)*
Characteristics: *In the Marbled Elephantnose, the upper and lower jaws form a trunklike mouth. In their African homeland, breeding is triggered by the rains, which swell the rivers and provide food for the youngsters. Elephantnoses are shy creatures and best kept only with their own kind.*

MARBLED BICHIR

Polypterus palmas palmas
Mature size: *30cm (12in)*
Characteristics: *Glossy scales like protective body plates; an eel-like body; not one dorsal fin but many, held erect like tiny flags. All this, plus tube nostrils and pectoral fins, which the creature seems to want to use more like legs, makes the bichir a real oddity of the fish world, and that is why it is sometimes kept. But beware – it is a predator, and its tankmates need to be big and robust. It hunts by night, locating its prey with tube nostrils (inset) that are capable of independent movement.*

DELHEZI'S BICHIR

Polypterus delhezi
Mature size: *35cm (14in)*
Characteristics: *From Zaire, in Africa, comes one of the more attractive bichirs. Like other members of the genus, it uses an adapted swimbladder to breathe atmospheric air and needs to surface every now and again to take a gulp. Otherwise, it spends most of its time resting on the bottom, looking unnervingly intelligent, as if waiting for an evolutionary quantum leap to pitch it onto land. Its scales are covered with a hard, laquer-like coating.*

SPOTTED GARPIKE

Lepisosteus oculatus
Mature size: *120cm (48in)*
Characteristics: *A survivor from the Jurassic Period (about 200-150 million years ago), this US citizen is a lurk predator that can really only be kept with its own kind in a large, planted tank. It will, however, learn to take dead food. With its shiny coat of primitive ganoid scales, it has a rather forbidding, sharp-nosed prehistoric charm – a modern Ichthyosaur.*

REEDFISH

Erpetoichthys calabaricus
Mature size: *40cm (16in)*
Characteristics: *This is the stretch limo among polypterids and, like the eel it rather resembles, is a great escape artist. The tube nostrils featured below are sensory organs that perform the same function as the barbels of catfish. Hard protective scales still allow huge flexibility, enabling the Reedfish to squeeze into quite small crevices or even burrow into the substrate. Although a predator, it is a danger only to bite-sized fish, and is peaceable with other members of its own species.*

Starting with the common goldfish, breeding by man has produced fancy goldfishes in a wide diversity of patterns, body forms and finnage. These coldwater fishes are either beautiful or bizarre. You decide.

Gaze into a tank of fancy goldfishes and be amazed at their diversity of form and coloration. Here a matt black Moor, trailing resplendent finnage and looking out on the world through boggling, telescopic eyes; there a Ranchu, its head adorned with a hood looking like a succulent raspberry. And resting on the bottom is a Calico Bubble-eye, so bizarre you would not imagine such a creature could exist, had you not seen it for real. These weird and wonderful creatures are all members of a single species, *Carassius auratus.*

The Chinese, and later the Japanese and Europeans, have been culturing fancy goldfish for centuries. The raw material is an innocuous little brown carp, a fish remarkable only for its hardiness. The 'fairground' goldfish is one stage removed from the ancestral type, a simple mutation of the skin into a bright golden-orange. These common goldfish are quite able to survive in a garden pond. Many of the varieties shown on the following pages, however, are not suited to the great outdoors; they are highly valued aquarium fish that richly deserve the pampering of their owners.

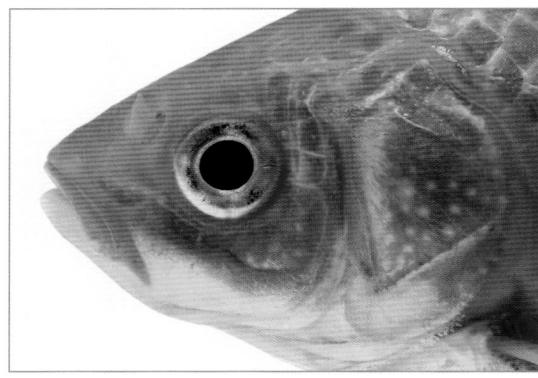

Males in breeding condition carry spawning tubercles on their gill plates.

Think of any anatomical characteristic, and chances are that fancy goldfish will carry them to extremes. Eyes, body shape, finnage and coloration have all been changed. There are matt and metallic goldfish in single and multi-patterned

Fantails are prime examples of twin-tailed manmade goldfish.

ISHES

A canary-yellow, rather than the usual orange, common goldfish.

Extreme fins, eyes and body shape – a Calico Globe-eye.

colorations. Some bear a tall, proud dorsal fin, while in others this fin is absent. Most fancies have twin tails, either short and stiff or flowing like a veil of delicate silk. Their palette makes the term 'goldfish' redundant, when selective breeding has led to so many other hues. And what are we to make of pompon nostrils, extravagant hoods, or a skin clothed in scales like the dimpling on a golf ball?

In common with toy dogs or lop-eared rabbits, fancy goldfish are there to be admired, although some of us will always prefer creatures 'as nature intended', with form tied in closely to function. But the need to swim fast from predators or be drably clad for protection no longer applies to fish that spend their lives among their own peaceable kind in aquariums. We should not try to attribute human emotions to them and imagine that a Moor or a Celestial (so named because its eyes are directed upwards to the heavens) is conscious of its appearance. As long as basic needs are met – good food and impeccable water quality – fancy goldfish will lead a life of simple contentment and provide endless enjoyment and fascination for their admiring keepers.

COMMON GOLDFISH

Carassius auratus
Mature size: *20cm (8in)*
Characteristics: *This fish has set many hobbyists on the road to keeping more exotic, tropical species – a childhood pet that would survive everything until its owner developed better fishkeeping skills. The Common Goldfish is closely related to the Crucian Carp (Carassius carassius) and will happily live in ponds, but first the Chinese, then the Japanese, worked on this chunky little carp to selectively breed fancy varieties. It is hard to appreciate that some of these are the same fish: the more extravagant the finnage, body shape, coloration and eye type, the less able these fancies are to live outdoors. Not so the world's most popular pet, the 'common' goldfish.*

SHUBUNKINS

Mature size: 15cm (6in)
Characteristics: It is mainly their coloration that sets Shubunkins apart from Common Goldfish – a suit of matt and nacreous scales in red, blue, orange, white and black. 'Pedigree' London (short-finned) and Bristol (long-finned) Shubunkins are less common than these 'everyday' varieties.

FANTAILS

Mature size: 20cm (8in)

Characteristics: Fantails, the western equivalent of the Ryukin, show an egg-shaped body, tall dorsal fin and a double tail, carried quite stiffly. This highly variable variety is available in all shades, metallic or nacreous, and with or without telescope eyes. The young fish to the left may lose the black pigment as they mature, although the way this carries on into the finnage suggests that in this instance it is a stable trait. Note the lack of a shoulder hump on all these examples. Fantails are tough, although prone to swimbladder trouble if chilled.

RED-AND-SILVER RYUKIN

Mature size: 20cm (8in)

Characteristics: The very deep-bodied Ryukin is a Japanese strain of fancy goldfish named after the Ryukyu Islands between Japan and Taiwan. The back slopes up steeply from a somewhat pointed head, and the single dorsal fin is carried proudly, adding to the impression of height. The caudal fin typically has four lobes, although three are also acceptable. This variety has normal eyes and no hood, and swims well, despite the extravagant finnage. All the usual varieties, including calico, are represented, but red-and-silver is the most prized.

CALICO RYUKIN

'Calico' describes goldfish marked with red, black, blue, white and orange. They are available with matt or metallic scales. These Ryukin are typical of the type, every bit as bright as koi, but requiring much less space to keep.

ORANDA

Mature size: 20cm (8in)

Characteristics: In Orandas, developed in Holland, the body is actually deeper than it is long. This can predispose the fish to swimbladder trouble, as that organ is compressed and foreshortened. The twin caudal fins resemble those of a Veiltail, and are ideally squared off, rather than forked, but the defining characteristic is the hood (or wen), composed of soft, wartlike growths. These take some time to develop, and in some examples never do, or only poorly. Typically, the hood starts on the top of the head and spreads over the cheeks and around the eyes. Coloration is highly variable, and black pigment in young red fish (shown here in the middle) is usually lost over time. The baby metallic veiltail-type Orandas shown at right are only nine weeks old.

A still-developing oranda hood. Newly emerging growths appear as white spots, not to be confused with the disease of that name.

RED-AND-SILVER
ORANDA

Mature size: 20cm (8in)

Characteristics: These mature Red-and-Silver Orandas show exceptionally good dorsal and tail finnage, which balances the very deep body. Note how the hood in the fish at the bottom of the page is almost covering the eyes. You can see how two or three Orandas kept together will give an ever-changing perspective of form, depending on the direction in which they swim.

RED METALLIC ORANDA

Mature size: 20cm (8in)

Characteristics: A red hood on a red fish shows the two shades that can result from the presence or absence of scales. On the metallic body, the coloration is toned down to more of an orange, while on the head, the wen is more crimson – because here, of course, there are no scales to reflect back the light. The Japanese call red 'Hi' and in koi and goldfish they recognize many more shades than a Westerner could begin to imagine.

REDCAP ORANDA

Mature size: 20cm (8in)
Characteristics: Looking like surprised Regency
aristocrats in red fright wigs, these fish are an example
of beauty in simplicity. The hood, unlike in other
Orandas, is confined to the top of the head, where
each warty element should be of equal size. The body
should be silver, and the finnage (here of the veiltail
type) pure white, with no red intruding.
Young fish with broad heads are
preferred, as this gives the most
room for the wen to develop.

RED-AND-BLACK GLOBE-EYE

Mature size: 10cm (4in)
Characteristics: The overall body shape is similar to that of the Veiltail, with a single dorsal fin and pointed tips to the other fins, all of which should be paired. The eyes protrude from the head – hence the variety name. The caudal fin should be forked to about a quarter of its length and about three-quarters of the body length. In good specimens, the eyes should be at the tip of truncated cone-shaped protuberances and should be symmetrical.

As the fish swims, the dorsal fin should be erect and the caudal fin should flow. The Globe-eye is also known as the Telescope-eye in the USA and the Dragon Fish in the Far East.

You can also find self (single) shade metallic, variegated or calico Globe-eyes. The calicos must be bright, with a blue background and brown, orange, red, yellow and violet patches, spotted with black.

MOOR

Mature size: 15-25cm (6-10in)

Characteristics: A Moor is a black Veiltail with globe-eyes, and although perfect examples are very hard to find, the variety is enduringly popular. You would think that such a short-bodied fish would lack grace, but the flowing single dorsal and other, paired, fins lend it an unlikely dignity, though it is not the fastest of swimmers. Ideally, Moors should be a uniform velvety black, but bronze scalation tends to show through with age. All fancies of this general shape require a deep tank (50cm/20in minimum). What is going on behind those unfathomable, dark eyes? Goldfish are popularly thought of as having an attention span of seconds – if so, how come they recognize their owners?

PANDA BUTTERFLY

Mature size: 15-25cm (6-10in)

Characteristics: Black-and-white chic in the animal kingdom is shared among magpies, skunks and, of course, giant pandas – after which this variant of the Moor is named. The silver-and-black pattern is highly variable, but when dark globe-eyes appear on a white face the illusion is complete. Other markings need not necessarily be symmetrical, but should balance out. The Butterfly name refers to the tail which, when viewed from above, reminds one strongly of the wings of a swallowtail. The twin caudal fins should be fully divided and spread.

RED BUTTERFLY MOOR

Mature size: 15-25cm (6-10in)
Characteristics: Moors are not always black, which is why the old name 'Black Moor' is still useful in describing those that are, even though purists will not use it. These fish, of course, are red, with only a touch of silver around the globe-eyes and below the chin, and they share with the Panda the butterfly-shaped twin tail. The tail is divided but not forked, in true Veiltail fashion.

BLACK
RANCHU

Mature size: 20cm (8in)
Characteristics: They could be mistaken for giant aquatic loganberries, but these Black Ranchu are superb examples of fancy goldfish that are prized as highly as koi by the Japanese, who refined them from the very similar Chinese Lionhead. The main difference is that the Ranchu's back arches more steeply down towards the fully divided caudal fin which, as a result, is carried downwards. Hood (wen) development is excellent in these matt-black beauties, extending over the top of the head and around the cheeks, almost (but not quite) covering the eyes. Ranchu are remarkably strong and hardy, and good swimmers.

RED-AND-SILVER METALLIC
RANCHU

Mature size: *20cm (8in)*
Characteristics: *Ranchu are bred in metallic self-coloration or combinations, as well as calico. The Red-and-Silver type is popular, as this gives the best possible contrast between the hooded head and the body. These fish are still juveniles, yet to fully develop the wen. The top view shows just how the tail should be configured. Note the smooth dorsal profile, with no suggestion of a vestigial fin. Rigorous culling is needed to maintain the breed standards, but a good Ranchu is a sight to behold, giving an impression of restrained power.*

These are nine-week-old Red Metallic Ranchu, in which the hoods are almost absent. Full development may take up to three years.

RED-AND-SILVER METALLIC
RANCHU

Mature size: 20cm (8in)

Characteristics: Red-and-Silver Ranchu are not just confined to the Sarasa type (red head, silver body); the twin coloration, as here, can flow in a more informal pattern that most resembles the markings on Kohaku, a type of koi. In the Jadehead, the face and hood are white and the rest of the fish is red-and-silver. There are also examples where the red extends along the back and is carried on into the finnage. Indeed, new variants are appearing all the time.

RED METALLIC
RANCHU

Mature size: 20cm (8in)

Characteristics: Sometimes, simplicity of coloration is the hardest thing of all to accomplish in a fancy goldfish. The tendency of all fishes is to have a dark back and a pale belly, the best camouflage against predators coming at them from above and below. Small wonder, then, that these Red Metallic Ranchu show areas of silver, too. They are still fine fish, the steeply angled backs being especially well pronounced. Hood development is not as extreme as in the Black Ranchu on page 194.

CHOCOLATE
POMPON

Mature size: 20cm (8in)

Characteristics: *Goldfish have paired nostrils, opening into a U-shaped tube lined with sensory cells that smell, and taste, the water. Each pair of nostrils is covered by a tiny flap of skin known as the nasal septum, but in Pompons these septa, or narial excrescences, have become exaggerated into fleshy balls that look rather like the tools of a cheerleader's trade. The bigger they are, the better – within reason. They should not be so large that they are sucked into the fish's mouth as it breathes. Pompons can be of the Fantail type, with a dorsal fin, or the Lionhead type, without. Good examples show a contrast in coloration between the nasal growths and the rest of the body. They occur in all the usual fancy goldfish hues.*

HAMA NISHIKI

Mature size: 20cm (8in)

Characteristics: A Hama Nishiki is actually a Pearlscale Oranda, with a spherical body and slightly longer fins than the true Oranda. Like that fish, it has a hood (wen) that covers only the top of the pointed head. Some examples also show pompons, so it is a bit of an allsorts fancy goldfish. It comes in several coloration patterns, metallic and matt-scaled. Should one of the domed scales be rubbed off accidentally, it will grow back as a normal scale, one reason for keeping show fish only with their own, sedate, kind.

PEARLSCALE

Mature size: 15cm (6in)

Characteristics: Breeders of fancy goldfish typically work on body shape, finnage, coloration and eye development. However, in the Pearlscale, another mutation involves the structure of the scales. Each is thickened in the centre with a deposit of calcium carbonate (chalk), which makes it stand proud, so the overall effect is of the dimples on a golf ball – very visible on the Hama Nishiki (opposite). Other characteristics are a rounded body, forked and divided tail fin carried high, and a rather dainty head and small mouth. These examples also have an Oranda-type hood. Calico Pearlscales are particularly attractive, and surprisingly hardy.

BRONZE <small>BUBBLE-EYE</small>

Mature size: 20cm (8in)

Characteristics: Little beauties or wobbly weirdos? There is no neutral territory of opinion with Bubble-eyes. Coloration is secondary to those huge, fluid-filled pouches, so this variety can be found in self (single) shades – bronze, as here, or red or yellow, or in various calico or metallic combinations. The pouches carry pigment and so they, too, can be of any coloration. In the paler types, blood vessels stand out on the bubbles, adding to the surreal effect. The twin tail should be deeply forked, and the dorsal fin is absent.

ORANGE
BUBBLE-EYE

Mature size: 20cm (8in)
Characteristics: These extreme fancy goldfish are not great swimmers, as the eye pouches tend to wobble in motion and make their owners head-heavy, so their usual resting place is on the tank floor. Take care not to include any sharp gravel or décor, as those bubbles can so easily be burst. In fact, this variety is best kept on its own, as it is not able to compete for food with more agile and better-sighted goldfish.

INDEX

ACKNOWLEDGMENTS

The publishers would like to thank the following hobbyists and aquatic stores for their invaluable help during the preparation of this book:

David and Paul Cummings at Kesgrave Tropicals, Ipswich, Suffolk.

Dave, Jason and Lewis at Swallow Aquatics, Colchester, Essex.

Richard Hardwick, Ivan Mogford and Wayne at Wharf Aquatics, Pinxton, Nottinghamshire.

Paul Sparks, Chris Dickerson and Mike Laws of the Thorpe Aquarist Society in the Norwich and Kings Lynn area.

Adrian Burge, Publicity Officer of the British Killifish Association.

Glen Bird and Dean at The Aquatic Warehouse, Enfield, Middlesex.

Brian Paddock and David Quelch at Waterworld, Enfield, Middlesex.

Andy Taylor at Britain's Aquatic Superstore, Bolton, Lancashire.

Neil Woodward, Clare, David and John at Pier Aquatics, Wigan, Lancashire.

Gareth Copping and Warren Hall at Shotgate Aquatics, Basildon, Essex.

Peter Hiscock, Steve and Emma at Maidenhead Aquatics, Crowland, Peterborough.

Pete Daniels, Hadleigh, Suffolk.

Colin and Kay Sargeant, Stowmarket, Suffolk.

Rachel, Jamie, Carol and James at Hertfordshire Fisheries, St. Albans, Hertfordshire.

Robin Moore at Knights Ivy Mill, Godstone, Surrey.

Maureen McGurk at Koishi, Tewin, Welwyn, Hertfordshire.

Dick Mills; Dennis Roberts; Derek Lambert.

The photograph of the adult Flower Horn Cichlid shown on page 30 is © Nathan Chiang, Taiwan.

And, of course, we must thank the fish, including the one that nearly got away! **Geoff Rogers**